"BI
"1 PAGE BRIEFS

BY

JAMES R SHAFER

THEOLOGY FOR MY GRANDKIDS IN PAGES, NOT CHAPTERS, OR A BOOK!

SCRIPTURE REFERENCES

<EXAMPLES>   <APPLICATIONS   <PLANNING>

FROM THE PAST   AT THE RESENT   FOR THE FUTURE

2021

Table of Contents

DEDICATION (2021)

The list I should put on this page is innumerable. Could I leave out my parents, my wife, my children, my pastors over the years, or my Christian friends over the country with whom I have studied, prayed, suffered, and shared?

But I've chosen my grandkids: Conner, Chelsea, and Chandler. And I thought if I could just share what I learned with them, in a simple, easy-to-read, set of "1 Page Briefs," then maybe they could digest something off of a page instead of reading an entire volume; well that was the goal. Then the briefs started streaming.

We had a fantastic 1st decade from Disneyland to Disneyworld. We also went from the Vail Ski Resort to the Pacific Ocean. I also had the pleasure of sending each of them to 2 years of church pre-school, so they could at least hear about Jesus and the Bible.

I watched them grow through their 2nd decades, and head out to work and college. My work took me miles away, but I got to stop by when I traveled through.

At this stage, my wife and I retired to Arizona, and for now, they're in Denver. I'm sure that will change before this decade is over. I also appreciate 2 retired old folks who aren't much worth visiting as they were in the past.

Anyway, I want to see my kids, and my GRANDKIDS someday in the arms of Jesus, and for that reason, I wish to share with them, in this manner, some "1 PAGERS" on what the Bible is all about.

God Bless You Kids; I love you (and all the rest of my relatives☺)

CHIP NOTES "1 PAGE BRIEFS" (2016-2021)

I write these "briefs" to visit some thoughts to my 3 grandchildren who each remind me, in an enormous way, of my high school and college years. They have each worked at their education and lives thus far, much in the same way as I did. So I'm going to share some thoughts with them, totally unsolicited, about facing life. Who knows? Maybe 2021 will be my last year (but it wasn't).

For 50 years now, I've been studying about my Creator. I visited ancestry.com recently and found no apes or gorillas in my past. I chose not to fantasize about billions of years to a point that my accidental parents slurped some primordial slime. I did however discover a great deal about being designed and created, seen in the womb, having the hairs on my body numbered, and a significant "life after" to glory or judgment, all based on buying that ticket in this life.

I've been studying this book called the Bible, or God's word, for over 50 yrs now. Don't criticize me if you haven't. It's loaded with items and chapters that explain this mess we call life, and states that it has been delivered and written by the author of life Himself. I was an above-average student throughout college. I was accepted at a law school in Chicago, but after 3 weeks, decided that another 3 years living at home just wasn't going to work. I got married and moved on. PS: we're still hitched! I did return for another year of post-grad at UCLA and a seminary where I improved into the "A" orbit.

As I script my thoughts at this 2016/2021 beginning, the world is in chaos. The world economy is crazy wild. The largest countries in the world owe each other trillions, and the 3rd world war seems to be erupting in the Middle East and its environs. The Bible actually details the final Big War as happening in the Middle East, and it kicks off after Israel becomes a nation again, which we have <u>now witnessed,</u>

So I'm going to share some reality with my grandkids as they begin this year. They don't need to change their lifestyles one bit. My point is to encourage them to include God in their thoughts, education, and lives, so they don't miss all the good things God has for them to enjoy (Ecclesiastes).

I think it's best summed up in the children's prayer I prayed 70 years ago: "if I should die before I wake, I pray the Lord my soul to take." I hope my friend that you join me in that prayer!

ACTIVATING MANLY/GODLY SAINTS

(2021)

This isn't my first rodeo. Heard that one before? As an old guy sitting near the back, I was overjoyed that over 150 men showed up for a fellowship breakfast at my church. That's a lot of men with a lot of faith! How do I know? Perform a survey across town, and check out the size of similar groups, and I think you'll agree. So the question arises, and the program is presented to activate these bodies, minds, and spirits.

I'm writing this particular brief because I'm keen on the 2nd point of the church trinity, which is FELLOWSHIP. One might suggest, as my friend Chris noted, that when we get to 25 participants, we could get more men activated with their spiritual gifts to perform the "work" of the ministry. Now we're at 150. Isn't that what Paul took note of in Ephesians 4 when he stated the purpose of teaching and pastoring is to equip believers for that work. (Ephesians 4:11)

We have an ambitious crowd of men and women at our church who attend men's and women's fellowship to numbers of 400+. Pastor Curtis laid out the outline program, to equip for that work. After the main get-together each month, he detailed 3 more steps of discipleship groups, mentors, and acts of service. Go get em' boys. He also maintained a strong Christian fellowship that must need benefit from a strong group of active men in the church.

All I'm suggesting, for the 1st step, is a return to what I believe helped build the men's ministry in the first place, back when I first came and Chris had that group of 25 men to work with. After beginning teaching, we went to the tables, and let the men all share their ideas at the table level so that we now had 25 men sharing, contributing, and learning from one another. We then would share back from a table and Chris would conclude. Now we have 150. ☺

This level of Koinonia, and sharing, will prime the pump for the follow-up activities detailed by Curtis for the group. I think you can sell more time-shares ☺ due to the active participation at the breakfast. My observation is a focused fellowship time that would be most productive for what you plan to accomplish, as opposed to another teaching/preaching session that is already admirably handled by Pastors Jon, Costi, and Daryl.

I know personally, that the main "joy" of my attendance now, is seeing and saying hello to men I saw every Sunday in the past, who I now only see once a month. GOOD FELLOWSHIP! Secondly, the opportunity to share with men at the table is an enormous benefit. Thirdly, the men get to share, hear from peers, and further dissect the designated speaker's contribution.

Anyway, I just had these thoughts to "Get back to the future." Every month we always have 20-30 new guys. If all the old ones ever came, we might have to flip some more pancakes. God always has a purpose for a growing church; its good fellowship, and strong ministries. Hopefully, it has good theology at the top of the pyramid, and we certainly are already getting that.

Thank you for your ministries!

AN ACTIVE CHURCH (2021)

It's fun being part of an active church. Over the years, my families have grown from childhood to adulthood in Christian fellowship. Of course, we have shared in school, work, sports, and neighborhood interaction, but a base Christian fellowship has always been there. Has the world in which we live changed; indeed. But Christ hasn't and neither has His Word. A lower percentage of people attend, fewer trust, fewer interact, and sadly in this country, fewer care much of anything beyond this life. God has set up myriad churches in this country for theology, fellowship, and ministry. This is one of those which is being designed to satisfy those needs for people. It will be very interesting for anyone who has a keen interest in God, and a keen interest in their neighbors (fellow men).

Ephesians 4, as listed, sets the base for this fellowship. We call it a Christian church. It says our Creator sets up the fellowship with teachers and 4 other roles to train us and love us. It also includes teaching us to love one another, care for one another, and 100 other "one anothers" as we begin the "work of the ministry." That is all we are gifted for, by God, to make the earth a better place to live, and for people, a better place to give to each other. We are then motivated to become one in love and grow and mature as a body.

Travel with us on this exciting journey to grow and develop as a fellowship of people who are a part of God's family. The applied truths of God's word are really exciting. The truth of where we came from, where we are, and where we are going, are even more exciting. Join us, enjoy with us, enjoy with us helping others, and enjoy your personal creation and God's total creation.

An added note to this timely framework: as we write this, the pandemic onslaught of Covid-19 is here. There has never been a better time to market the truth of God's love to the end of fellowship and ministry for Christians, and also salvation for the lost. People are stressed and concerned and open as never before in my brief existence. After decades of living for the present, in our society, mankind is considering the future in earnest.

Our sharing will be timely

God Bless

AN ACTIVE CHURCH

Ekklesia

An Action-Oriented Fellowship

Ephesians 4:11-16

[11] And he gave the apostles, the prophets, the evangelists, the shepherds[a] and teachers,[b] [12] to equip the saints for the work of ministry, for building up the body of Christ, [13] until we all attain to the unity of the faith and of the knowledge of the Son of God, to mature manhood,[c] to the measure of the stature of the fullness of Christ, [14] so that we may no longer be children, tossed to and fro by the waves and carried about by every wind of doctrine, by human cunning, by craftiness in deceitful schemes. [15] Rather, speaking the truth in love, we are to grow up in every way into him who is the head, into Christ,[16] from whom the whole body, joined and held together by every joint with which it is equipped, when each part is working properly, makes the body grow so that it builds itself up in love.

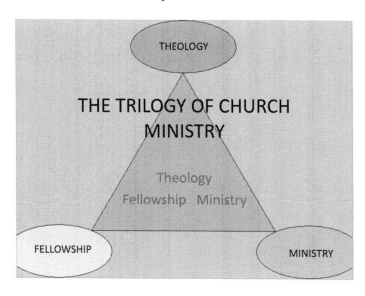

GOD'S WORD (BIBLE) AS FOUNDATIONAL (THEOLOGY)

Apostles and Prophets

ll Timothy 3: 16,17

[16] All Scripture is breathed out by God and profitable for teaching, for reproof, for correction, and for training in righteousness, [17] that the man of God[b] may be complete, equipped for every good work.

FOR BY GRACE ARE YOU SAVED

Ephesians 2: 8,9

Theology

[8] For by grace you have been saved through faith. And this is not your own doing; it is the gift of God,

FELLOWSHIP

Koinonia

Love One Another

Agape'

1 John 4 : 7-12   God Is Love

[7] Beloved, let us love one another, for love is from God, and whoever loves has been born of God and knows God. [8] Anyone who does not love does not know God, because God is love. [9] In this the love of God was made manifest among us, that God sent his only Son into the world, so that we might live through him. [10] In this is love, not that we have loved God but that he loved us and sent his Son to be the propitiation for our sins. [11] Beloved, if God so loved us, we also ought to love one another. [12] No one has ever seen God; if we love one another, God abides in us and his love is perfected in us.

FELLOWSHIP

On Sunday, we heard of Philemon's story of applied love. Paul, steeped in theology, entered the dominion of application. How does one apply their theology, if not through application? Please note the added names that met in his home as a small Koininia group.

In the scripture of Philemon 4-7, Paul takes note of Philemon's love and the fellowship in his life and asks him to apply it to Onesimus, an ex-slave who had run away and wished to return.

Fellowship then should be the application and growth of one's theology, a separate point of the Christian triangle, to expand on the teaching point of theology. In this process, as the recipients of the Elders theology, give, in the process of Koininia and loving one another

MINISTRY

The Gifts of the Spirit Applied

and Assigned by God

Romans 12

I Corinthians 12

Gifts of Grace

[3] For by the grace given to me I say to everyone among you not to think of himself more highly than he ought to think, but to think with sober judgment, each according to the measure of faith that God has assigned. [4] For as in one body we have many members,[e] and the members do not all have the same function, [5] so we, though many, are one body in Christ, and individually members one of another. [6] Having gifts that differ according to the grace given to us, let us use them: if prophecy, in proportion to our faith; [7] if service, in our serving; the one who teaches, in his teaching; [8] the one who exhorts, in his exhortation; the one who contributes, in generosity; the one who leads,[f] with zeal; the one who does acts of mercy, with cheerfulness.

SHARE THE WORD
(WITH OTHERS)

Ministry

Go therefore and make disciples of all nations...

Matthew 28:19

Go therefore and **make disciples** of all nations, baptizing them in the name of the Father and of the Son and of the Holy Spirit,

ASSURANCE AND INSURANCE (2021)

Assurance is something you hope for, looking forward in life. Insurance is something you purchase to protect you in case your assurances don't work out. ☺ We are encouraged to "draw near to God with a sincere heart in full ASSURANCE of faith" (Hebrews10:19-25). In that same paragraph, well worth reading, we are encouraged to NOT give up meeting together so we can encourage one another.

This begs the question; can we really grow in faith without fellowship? Have you ever known anyone who seems to have grown older, but never grown up? There is a trilogy for growth that I have mentioned earlier:

Theology

Fellowship   Ministry

These topicals lead to growth and maturity. Maturity leads to assurance, and voiding the above, leads to the need for insurance. I trust this gives you a picture of maturity for a believer with stronger faith and fellowship. Of course, good Theology is a mandate. The key "ROCK" of faith is also the gospel which holds the trilogy together.

Outsiders can get confused when Christians divide on Charisma vs non-Charisma. Confusion sets in on baptism, but not communion. And when, of course, you bring in the subject of the end times and the future, according to Scripture, we can really look discombobulated to non-believers. The monkey wrench gets thrown in at the last, by cults who follow leaders down some rabbit trail regarding God and Jesus. Don't mess with my Jesus! He is the son of God making Him equal with God (John 5:18). He was the "Creator of the World" (Colossians 1:16). He is the "Alpha and the Omega" (Revelation 1:8).

14

Have you ever bought an insurance policy? It can be an investment. It can be a gamble. It's meant to cover costs that occur or expenses that happen, that need economic replacement. Investing in God's program is an unction created by God's Spirit in a particular fellowship. It's an investment in ministry to serve and help others in need. "God loves a cheerful giver" (2 Corinthians 9:7). Helping others in need is the greatest pleasure in this life. It's the greatest pleasure of the materially blessed!

So read the instruction manual, until satiated (The Bible)! Join a regular group of fellow believers   (Fellowship), and give until it hurts; cheerfully (Ministry). From these actions and activities, you will have the assurance of faith and a relationship with your Creator. You can deposit your insurance payment in the offering plate.

I recommend, in this case, you get "whole" insurance! ☺

ATTRIBUTES OF GOD

To consider Godly attributes, seems to be an effort to pigeonhole our Creator and Savior into something we can digest or comprehend. The God of the Universe is so inscrutable; He had to become a person to us to give us perspective for attachment. It's amazing!

I read that the Elders under Moses wanted to see God and requested to join Moses up the mountain. God allowed this and the 70 Elders saw God's feet. (Exodus 24) The apostle Thomas wanted to see Christ in the flesh, in order to believe, and he did. (John 20)

Do I need the same thing, or can I just believe? I've chosen the latter. I now believe that God is the Creator, I know now that God is Love. And lastly, the Bible tells me that God is eternal. The great "I AM."

This gives me a launching pad. I can now search further and see what believing Christian scholars have learned before me. I see many opinions and applications of the faith out there today.

I want to learn the Gospel; the reality of the gospel, and the promise of the gospel (1 Corinthians 15). Christ died for me? Why? I ACCEPT! Help me now to live it out. I hope to learn more and more about God... but not to squeeze Him into my brain. I wish to expand my world and consciousness into His Kingdom

PRAISE GOD

ATTRIBUTES OF GOD

At this stage of growth, my three focused attributes are:

1) Creator
2) Love
3) Eternal

"God is the Creator "of the universe and life that exists on it; Genesis 1 says it all. There is a beginning that He started, and you could say it's time and life. He needed six days, according to Genesis 1 and Exodus 20, and if the Bible says it, I accept it. He didn't need BB's of years or experimentation. He knew exactly what He wanted!

We create cell phones, babies, civilizations, governments, etc. It's always something created out of something. We create better things out of weaker things (hopefully). We extend human life with medicine, repairs, and replacement.

The God of the Bible (and the world) creates something out of nothing. Hebrews 11:3 "what is seen was not made out of things that are visible."

"God is Love" 1 John 4 explains it all, or maybe it's inexplicable? He is giving; He creates, maintains, and secures. He doesn't need us, but He's created us, and continues to serve us. THAT'S LOVE!

"God is Eternal." Psalm 90: 2 and that concept can't be defined or framed by us lowly arthropods. He has always existed; He will never not exist. Deuteronomy 33:27 "The Eternal God."   I'm created. I have a beginning. I've been promised my existence will be forever, but it's dependent on Him. John 3: 16

NOW THAT'S LOVE, AND IT'S ETERNAL!

ATTRIBUTES OF GOD

It's difficult to assign any attachment to the creator of the universe, from electrons and DNA, to the stars of the solar system. Nonetheless, I'm assigned.

I'm a fairly new Christian. To put it simply, something happened in my life that spoiled my nicely laid-out and controlled projections of happiness and splendor. I was exceedingly disappointed. Then, Jesus stepped in!

I'm now eternally grateful, as I step up and learn who God is, and why He saved me. I must add, based on what I've learned, and felt, I would rather have faced my disappointments and been saved, then to have been joyfully existing in this life without salvation.

I can now see what creation and the Creator is all about. Why didn't I learn this years ago? As the saying goes, "better late than never." ASSUREDLY, I now want to know more, and studying His attributes seems to be a good step forward, a place of education and a great starting point.

Who is God? Please lead me, Jesus!

BE AN OVERCOMER 2021

There are 7 churches listed in the Book of the Revelation in the Bible. I believe God is presenting a picture of what is and what is to come. Pastor Darryl addresses these fellowships as cool, suffering, worldly, compromising, dead, obedient, and finally apostate. I'll let Darryl complete the details. You might also read chapters 2 and 3 yourself. They are all different, but they all have two things in common. It's the common that we will be focusing on.

Each of the churches is "called out" (Ecclesia), and each has "overcomers." Some expositors see these churches as contemporary to John's (the authors) lifetime. Some expositors also see these churches as an overview of the last 2000 years and a picture of the developing Christian church down through the ages. For this "Briefs" purpose, it's not a hill to die on.

Each of these fellowships, then, were called out to come together by God. Christ warned us 30-60 years earlier that the "church" would contain wheat and tares. He warned us to not cut out, remove, or destroy the tares in fellowship, as we might cut out the wheat in the process. So if you are called to Christian fellowships, enjoy the teaching, enjoy the fellowship, and by all means, be active in ministry. God has picked you with purpose, for purpose, to purpose. Spending an excessive amount of time purging the tares isn't Biblical.

The Second word of consistency is "overcomers." Who is this group? 1 John 5:5 defines them. "Who is it that overcomes the world? It's only the one who believes that Jesus is the Son of God." In John 5, the Pharisees sought to crucify Christ based on His testimony of being God's Son. So not every person called out is actually saved, I guess? I love the old story when D L Moody was going to England to evangelize. One old pastor asked if Moody thought he had a monopoly on the Holy Spirit. A young pastor at the meeting replied in the negative and stated, "but the Holy Spirit has a monopoly on D L Moody ☺.

I personally feel that some people are "religious" Christians. Maybe their mom and dad took them to church. Maybe they took the kids to church. But in their hearts, they never exercised true belief and trust in who Christ is.

19

Maybe they feel no tug to be baptized as the Scripture exhorts multiple times? John 3 states: "You must be Born-Again."

To "overcome," then in each of the churches gains the privilege of: eat from the tree of Paradise, avoid the 2nd death, eat the hidden manna, get authority, get white garments, be a pillar in the temple, and sit on God's throne! WOW! That's a pile of payoffs for us winners. Get on the winning team, my friend.

If you've been "called out" (ecclesia), then be an overcomer.

Repent and be baptized. Don't wait! ☺

BEARING FRUIT: THE BELIEVER TEST 2021

150 years ago, life wasn't so easy. If you had to go, it was a walk out to the outhouse. Drinking water came from a well if you were mildly prosperous. The crops grew or died if God sent or withheld the rain. If you wanted a hamburger, there was only "slow" food, not "fast" food. And, of course, there wasn't any refrigeration to keep food from spoiling.

My, what we take for granted in the 2000s. Is our faith lived out the same way? As recently as my childhood, our faith was only presented at Sunday school and Church. In my small Michigan town, the church was the location for Theology, Fellowship, and Ministry. Today, one can meander to the TV chair and get all the Theology possible. If not there, just turn on the cell phone and u-tube any pastor/teacher in existence.

In previous briefs, I've listed the TFM of faith. Our trinity for belief must include, therefore, Fellowship and Ministry. We have an active faith to demonstrate our belief. We aren't supposed to be a stay-at-home crew, as God uses us to spread the Good News. In a study this past week, we heard a teaching on John 15:1-8. These first 8 verses cover what Jesus Christ says as He compares us to fruit trees. If your faith is real, you produce fruit. I have a lemon tree out back, and I know that because it grows lemons each year.

Christ notes that if you truly believe, you will produce. As you do produce, He will prune you, and increase your production. Sadly, according to John 15, if you don't produce, He will cut you off and burn the dead branches. He also covers this in Luke 13 with the example of the fig tree. The planted tree goes 3 years without producing figs. The owner said to cut it off as it's taking up space. The vineyard manager asked to fertilize the fig tree and give it another year. Do you need another year?

Get the message? There are dead, non-producing Christians who may need another year, if indeed they are a Christian. It's a scary premise that you are a "religious" Christian who was never Born Again; in the Spirit. Over the years, I have heard numerous testimonies of churchgoers, choir members, or TV watchers who realized they needed to repent and be changed radically, in the Spirit; and they did! What is your fruit? How much do you produce? Are you prune-able?

Don't be cut off as Christ spoke of. Get in some active fellowship. Be a part of a/some ministries.

It's never too late! Especially, if you're reading this.

SO YOU WANT TO KNOW WHAT THE BIBLE IS ALL ABOUT?

I began my venture of study some 50 years ago, and I'm not quite finished☺. I did discover 3 basic studies that covered it for me, and I will pass them on. I call them the three tens: God's commandments for the perfect life, His system for giving, and 10 chapters which show you, from where you came, how we fell away from our Creator's plan for us, and how we can return(as you have), and where it's (life) all headed.

1) The first ten set is called the 10 Commandments. They're listed in Exodus 20. When you read them, you realize you'll never obey them entirely, or continually. In James 2:10, God writes that if you break one, you're guilty of all of them.WOW, demanded perfection! That's why we need God's forgiveness. I don't care if you lie, steal, want (covet) your neighbors "stuff," or just dishonor your father and mother. YOU NEED TO BE SAVED.

2) The 2nd ten involves giving. There are many examples of unselfish giving; as God wants us to learn that all that we have is a gift, and portions of what we have, need to be given away to help others. This area involves tithes and offerings. A tithe is like tax. It's many 10%'s. Offerings are over and above. The key is to share and give. We live in a rich culture and economy, taking credit for all we earn. Biblically, the Bible leads us/commands us to share what we've earned. God destroyed a city once for not giving to the poor and needy: Ezekiel 16:49. He doesn't ask for quantity; check out the "widows mite" (Luke 21:1-4). He's looking at attitude!

3) The third ten, then, are 10 chapters which you can read as you begin to learn God's Word. This is cool. Read the first 3 chapters of the Bible Genesis 1-3, and God details His Creation. The Bible says, He did it in six days (not 13 billion years), and He created man out of the dust and didn't just upgrade him from a gorilla. The next 3 to read are John 1-3 in the NT. After reading how Adam fell away back in Genesis (and blew it as our representative), we read about who God is, who Jesus Christ is, and how we can be reconciled to our Creator. Very nice! Lastly, where is this all going? You've heard about heaven, of course, and it's described in the last 2 chapters of the Bible. But read the last 4 chapters because God has to exercise

a little(or a lot of) judgment just before that, and some, understandably, don't make it to heaven.

So there we have it. A simple 1,2,3 for getting started in God's Word. When you've read the rules, you can see the need for forgiveness. When you begin a new attitude toward giving, you better appreciate what you've been given. When you begin to read/study God's book, you get the whole picture. There's a lot of filler in between to learn about, but you have days, weeks, months, or years to make that trip

One last thought. What's the Bible all about? The Good News! It's called the Gospel! You can find it explained in 1st Corinthians 15. Yes, Jesus died for our sins, and that is spectacular. But even more, He returned alive again to show us His victory over death. He then promised that to us if we would only be sorrowful over our sins and trust in Him. I guess you will experience that as you read this. Enjoy your studies. I'll see you in paradise ☺
GOD BLESS
ENJOY

BLESS YOUR FEET 2021

Seriously? Bless one's feet? Paul's epistles compare ministry to the body, and its use and sacrifice. In 1 Corinthians 12, he lists the body parts in comparison to the Spiritual gifts. But one's feet? As I approach my 9th decade, my foot thoughts turn to neuropathy, unfortunately. The nerve deterioration sets in, and the feet numb up. Maybe that just makes me better appreciate Paul's blessing toward those who keep moving.

I think of my current pastors whose feet have run from California, Colorado, and other states to share the Gospel and its teachings in this area. I've been so blessed in my latter days with men of pedigree and determination. It's nothing new, but I continue to get blessed. As Paul stated: "How beautiful are the feet of those who preach the good news" (Romans 10:15). He's referring to Nahum's verse: "Behold upon the mountain, the feet of him who brings good news," or in Isaiah "How beautiful upon the mountains are the feet of him who brings good news" (Isaiah 52:1).

This is an amazing picture to me. Paul doesn't say how blessed the man sitting on his butt all day watching TV is. Excuse my crudeness, but the great temptation in our society during this season of life, is to withdraw and have the entertainment brought in. As a child, the church was a social center. TV was just beginning, no cell phones, and the church was where people met and socialized. Today, that seems ancient. But the concept of an active body part still holds true.

Which body part is unnecessary? When I view fellow humans who have lost body parts in war, who can't see, can't hear (like half of my friends), or can't walk, I appreciate the different functions and their importance. Paul works out that equation in 1 Corinthians 12, and stresses the importance of church management and ministry. Each body part has a function, contributing to the whole. I don't take this lightly in my evaluation of the church family/community. It's not strong teaching without fellowship. It's not strong fellowship without ministry. And it's rarely strong ministry without good teaching.

So three cheers for the feet! God said it to the faithful of old, and repeated it through the disciples of the "New." Thank God for the ministers who massage their feet. The ones who take the Gospel forward from the mountain tops and spread the Word. Pray for them, support them, thank them, and be blessed.

As Paul continued: "So faith comes from hearing, and hearing by the Word of Christ" (Romans 10:17). Thank God for those who arise, move their feet, and get the Gospel out.

As some astute pastor once said: "don't ask God to guide your steps, if you're not moving your feet." (Maybe that was in the book of James ☺)

BLOOM WHERE YOU'RE PLANTED 2021

This seems to be an unquestionable issue in the plant world. It may be soft for a ledge in the Midwest, cactus in the desert or giant redwoods near the West coast. But with people, it is different. Or is it? We are so mobile, and especially today in our country and with modern transport, where the average person moves from job to job, vacations from time to time, and rarely physically ends up where they started.

Sunday, I was viewing one of the TV evangelists who was stressing this concept. His illustrations involved Joseph, Jeremiah, and his father. Without detail, it's obvious that Joseph had anything but control over his life's destiny. He was planted and uprooted again and again. Jacob's favored son was ordained by God, and his life is detailed in Genesis 37+. His brothers' betrayed him, and he was sent to rot in jail, yet his faith was emboldened, and he eventually was made a ruler over Egypt.

Jeremiah was a weeping prophet. He lived through the Babylonian invasion, and foresaw Israel's restoration. He even purchased property during the exile to ensure his grandchildren would prosper when his people returned to God's chosen land. He was a man of God's faith who planted his faith in God's future, believing God had a plan for them (Jeremiah 29:11),

Lastly, THE TV PREACHERS dad led a church to a congregation of 1000, only to be asked to leave. He and his wife then bought an old storefront with fewer than 100 people, and pastored it for the next 10 years. It then grew to 6000, his unlearned son took over, and it became the largest Christian ministry today. They go into the world and have drilled over 800 water wells in 3rd world countries, saving millions from drought, but mostly from death. All this and much more ministry to share the GOSPEL and gain salvation for the lost.

What if these individuals had continually asked for or activated a transplant? What if they hadn't "bloomed where they were planted"? This individual on TV ended by asking viewers to repent and ask for Christ's forgiveness. That's the message at my church. He finished by telling them to find a Bible-believing church and "get planted" ☺

If you have experienced that, in Christ, get planted. Get active and grow. Make Christian friends, and create synergy. The energy of synergy in

LOVE, leads to ministry. That's what we're here for (Ephesians 4). Create a beautiful flowerbed where you are. You never know what God has planned any more than Joseph, Jeremiah, or this TV pastor.

BLOOM WHERE GOD HAS PLANTED YOU!

BUTTERFLIES AND COCOONS...2021

One of the most beautiful transformations known in Creation is that of a caterpillar becoming a butterfly. The science of the metamorphosis process is quite amazing, as an ugly crawling herbivore creates a soft shell around itself and emerges as one of the most beautiful insects known to mankind over the next few months.

The process, however, is not a big party time for the emerging beauty bug. With a whole lot of significant struggle, the butterfly emerges, stretches, and is able to fly away in part because of the strength they gained in the process (kinda like birth, huh?). A person witnessed this process once, and as the story goes, he decided to help the emerging beauty. He cut open the cocoon with scissors, but the butterfly immediately emerged and fell to the ground. It seems that God had a purpose in strengthening the butterfly for significant flight.

Whatever strength is developed, it's a known fact that some butterflies migrate from Africa to England, and return. They can fly up to 3000 feet and reach speeds of 30 MPH. The process then, which has been tracked to 9000 miles for some, leads to their heavenly (skyward) reward. Are you beginning to see the analogy? Are we in a process of development and strengthening? Do we need (have to have) that process to fly away at the end? I believe Christ demonstrated that at the Cross. Are you living to skip the process? Do you wish to have someone cut your cocoon open? It just won't work.

A butterfly has but one short life of beauty while we are promised one for eternity. But we are asked to accept the process created by the Cross. How could the God-man go through the cocoon of Golgotha if it weren't the design of God, the Creator, as a process to save us eternally? Any other shortcut is, and has been proven to be, a waste of time. We know we all die! Daniel agrees in chapter 12, but shares that we will all awake to eternity; some to eternal bliss (a butterfly), and some to eternal condemnation. The Jehovah Witness religion missed this, and is busy trying to snip cocoons open for people.

Take it to your Spiritual bank, dear reader: "you must go through the process." Join me, with hopefully your friends and family, for that emergence. Don't just look for a life of fun, frivolity, and riches at this point (although some are OK as I'm not a stick in the mud; and neither is God), but covet the metamorphosis process.

It's the God-Ordained path to eternal bliss ☺

CAST YOUR NET! It's never too late 2021

So they were finished. Back to work. The Messiah had been killed, their status and protection gone, so why not return to Galilee from whence they had come three years ago, and do what they knew and had lived off of for their entire lives? Christ said He would meet them back in Galilee, but just like all of His prognostications, teachings, and prophecies, it went right over their heads.

I have friends that don't get it. They just trudge on, getting the most they can out of this life, hoping it will last longer, seeing the Dr., taking pills, having surgery, removing cataracts; need I go on? When I do, however, broach the subject of life ending, they go blank or just get angry. That's why I have and like my church friends. It's not because they are necessarily friendlier, more hospitable, or don't get angry, but rather, they have a real hope for a heavenly future, and the JOY of salvation and eternal life with our Creator.

A major part of Christ's return was to establish the earthly team He had set up for the ministry of the church. He had spoken of, and prophesied that He would be raised from the tomb and be replaced. Replaced? Yes, by the Holy Spirit who would miraculously enter the Spirits of believers, for inspiration, belief, and action, in this world. The rest is history. These under-educated fishermen became God-fearing giants, in a world which was in total rebellion to our Creator. These are just Biblical facts.

So the disciples were done. There are only so many hours to fish, as I understand the program, when the water is cool at the surface. That time had expired, and they were done. Christ approached and said, "cast your nets on the other side of the boat" And so, they complied. The nets filled, and they couldn't pull the catch in. Their eyes were suddenly opened, and they proclaimed "MASTER" Isn't that just like us? What does it take? Compliance!!! Actually, it's God-fearing compliance!

Could Christ just have stuck around, conquered the Romans, set up in the temple, and ruled? OF COURSE. But that's not His program. He passed on the mantle of God the Holy Spirit, and multiplied the ministry from 1 to 12 to 3000. Get it. With the Spirit of God in believers, He distributed offices of Pastors, Teachers, Evangelists, and Prophets. He then gave the gifts in 1 Corinthians 12 and Romans 12, for the work of the ministry. Just like the unregenerate disciples, unfortunately, we fight and quarrel, over which gifts are applicable, relevant, important, or real.

Cast your net on the other side today. Let God fill it now. Get it? You cast, He fills.

May God Bless your obedience and ministry!

CHURCH: MOVIE THEATRE OR FELLOWSHIP

The other day, I went to see a movie about a crusty old man who suffered (?) from dementia. It seemed terribly close to reality, but that's a brief saved for later. As we left the theatre with all the other theatre-goers, it crossed my mind that I experienced the same thing each Sunday as I entered and left my church. Rush in, rush out. I see a few people I know, ever so briefly, even though I love seeing them, but weekly.

I have shared in other briefs the trinity of church interaction. It includes theology, fellowship, and ministry (missions). The peak of the triangle is good (or great) theology, but the other two elements are equally important. I don't expect fellowship at the theater, but I crave it as a Christian. The combination of the aforementioned two will lead to the 3rd (ministry), of course. The next question, then, is, how does a church create the atmosphere and action of, and for, fellowship?

You need to catch people when they are there. You need to strike, as it's said, when the iron is hot. Children's Sunday school is concurrent with the church because that's when they're there. We don't say "come back Tuesday evening because we have more parking."

We have an open gym/arena at our church grounds where tables could be set, and people could share, and meet and greet, and one thing could lead to another. Years ago, the idea arose to have small groups for Christian fellowship other than Sunday AM. Over the years (we did it 50 yrs ago), it has flourished, and today is a mainstay for fellowship in any active church fellowship.

A church's most active Christians crave fellowship. It's an escape from the week-to-week forced interaction of work. Gainful activities (work) feed the kitty for sustenance but force the interaction with the non-believers where we need the strength to live and serve and share. A weekly lesson of learning and teaching builds the strength needed to support that effort. Mix it all together with fellowship, and it helps to cement the message and motivation for life's activities.

In our current facility, we have a large room and gym, which could be set for that interaction. People could join in sharing and fellowship during a church hour. We already serve coffee and donuts (God bless those people and that ministry), so they could be enjoyed in a sharing environment. The average "theatre go-er" can't realize the enormity of tasks and work that goes into making Sunday Morning flow. God Bless the workers! This idea is intended to increase that opportunity. The point is to grow the arena of fellowship, a major dimension of the church trinity.

The results are obvious: friends could meet and share at church facilities, and new attendees could break-in at a table level with a few others. Names could be learned! As with all fellowships, we have a season. Can we maximize that season? Can we champion this ministry and assignment? Can we enjoy it to the max and produce the most benefit for the most in need?

Will we just shuffle out at the end of the weekly movie as the world does after enjoying the show? Or

CAN WE BETTER EQUIP THE SHEEP FOR THE WORK OF THE MINISTRY?

CHURCH BUILDING ONE ANOTHER 2021

In an earlier brief, we covered the potential of church fellowship and its importance in the trinity of the church (ecclesia). This is a follow-up on that potential and the marked assistance in the attendees' growth, maturity, and service. As a reminder, we will show the trinity again:

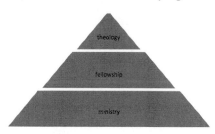

As important as good/great theology is, fellowship is the vehicle to applying theology and the process to ministry. Because, or due to, human constraint, church groups tend to focus on one of the points, or the other. It's just the same with the Trinity, if you will. This is demonstrated in denominations. Some overwhelm with teaching and education (my way or the highway), some emphasize fellowship, sharing, social action, etc., and some shoot out to ministry around the world.

I have attended, belonged to, and been a servant leader in, at least 15-20 churches in my life. This is, for the most part, due to family moves, career moves, or just basic moves. I'm still looking for the perfect ecclesia. Jesus had 7 variations that He listed/observed in Revelation 2 and 3. They did, however, have one thing in common; by attending, you could end up as an overcomer. So regardless of the trinity emphasis, if the Gospel was the basis of the theology, repenting, getting forgiven, and being baptized, were available experiences? After that, well……..

The point of this brief, then, is to change the format from a transplanted movie theatre to a house of "one-anothers." Did you realize the New Testament has about 100 "one-anothers" listed? You can Google it for the details. For example, in Matthew 28:19, Christ gives the disciples their marching papers. However, throughout the Epistles, we are exhorted, as today's disciples, to live out our salvation/forgiveness by "loving one another." Get it?

I propose that this can begin in the household where all God's Temples gather/collect each week. Our greatest friendships have come from these enclaves. I remember specifically Sunday School classes where fellow

Christians desiring more knowledge would gather. I think, more significantly, we wanted fellowship. The idea here is to get them when they are already gathered. Got rooms? Use them! Maybe a class-sized room, or maybe a large room with tables, sofas, easy chairs etc.

This is nothing new, my fellow churchgoers; it's a great fellowship time. So review the 100 "one-anothers" again. Can that fellowship activity start on Sunday morning? Can that richly generated process develop friendships, and process to ministry? It's not speculation, my friend; it's EXPERIENCE. Implement this program, and observe "moviegoers" become "equipped saints" (Ephesians 4:12) and agents of ministry as they start and continue to fellowship in church, in homes, and in their communities.

God Bless! ☺

CHURCH GROWTH AND MANAGING
GOD'S ASSETS (2021)

Each Sunday, our pastor prays for another Christian church in the area that's preaching the gospel. The lesson learned is that we share the wealth of knowing Jesus at our houses, but all have different-looking lawns. "LAWNS"? Let me guide you to the parable of the sower in Matthew 13. We all are working with different soils, causing or inhibiting growth.

The ministry of membership is to do the work of the gospel. See the book of James. The ministry of Leadership is to train us, Ephesians chapter 4. The GROWTH of individual churches is up to God. I Corinthians 3 says: "God who gives the growth." We, humans, tend to be, and ARE people-followers. In 1 Corinthians 1, Paul notes the followers of Paul, Apollos, Cephas, and, of course, CHRIST. He exhorted them to be unleashed as man-followers but rather, GOSPEL followers.

I remember the story of the young pastor in Iowa visiting his new flock. After a dozen visits to the farms of his congregants, he turned down a ½ mile road, lined with white picket fences, to a beautiful farmhouse with a full-length porch displaying rocking chairs. He saw the cattle grazing on the North side and acres of corn to the South. He was overwhelmed with the beauty, fastidiousness, and grandeur he viewed. He immediately broke into Praise for God's blessing to this farmer and all that God had done for him. When he finished his mini praise message 5 minutes later, the old farmer glibly replied, "yeh, I guess that's all true, but ya should have seen the place when He had it all to Hisself"!

And therefore, it seems, we are to be energized as caretakers for the true force of whatever "growth" our fellowship experiences. Back in the old farmer days, a couple hundred years, one might have a buggy or maybe a wagon. One powered that vehicle with the appropriate horsepower; sometimes an old nag; sometimes Clydesdales. There is no question that a Clydesdale pulled wagon must be spectacular.

The same can be noted for lawns. How one manicures their space can determine a spectacular view or a weed-infested eyesore (or earsore). One key job is to dig out and pull the weeds. Yes, the most beautiful lawns exist in part, because someone minds the weeds. The lawn must be fed and watered, however, and managing God's assets requires a shepherd capable of leading the flock to "green pastures" and beside still waters. Psalm 23.

History is replete with successful fellowships which exist and also have passed away. A church (ecclesia) needs excellent THEOLOGY, great FELLOWSHIP, and strong MINISTRIES. I've illustrated and discussed the concept in other renderings. The 2nd two chapters of Revelation detail the potential downfalls of all gatherings. The goal is always to be an Overcomer/conqueror. Is growth exciting? Yes. Is strong fellowship enjoyable? Absolutely! Is powerful ministry exhilarating? Immensely!

CHURCH IN THE WORLD, OR THE WORLD IN THE CHURCH   2021

A real challenge today is to approach a world that has gone haywire, as they say, but further. I was taught six decades ago to read our country's Declaration of Independence only to find we were endowed "BY OUR CREATOR" with life, liberty, and the pursuit of happiness. Now that we have evolved into a politically, Godless government, people take credit in the nation's capital for that freedom, but unfortunately take it away slowly, but surely.

Throughout our country's centuries, the Judeo/Christian church has helped to formulate laws, gratuities, and punishments based on applying God's Laws to society. Don't lie, steal, murder, and Love God as your Creator and sustainer. Honor your parents (for long life), and don't look over your fence all the time jealous of your neighbor's net worth, cars, or his wife. It seemed to work very well for a couple hundred years. As we enter the 2000s, it seems as though things have turned upside down.

We are commanded to "Go therefore and make disciples of all nations/peoples" (Matthew 28:19), which is more than running around with a sales pitch to join the "team." It involves learning the rules and helping society to benefit in their application. At the same time, we are admonished not to "love the world (system), or the things in the world" (1 John 2:15). That last one is hard in modern U.S.A suburbia.

Becoming a pastor in my early life amounted to a vow of poverty. My grandpa had to raise a cow and chickens to survive. My parents couldn't afford a car and lived in a home that the church owned (parsonage). Today pastors accumulate millions, own their own homes, and travel the world gratis. I'm not criticizing, but noting major changes that can significantly change attitudes.

Keep in mind that it's the "love of" that counts. Are we affecting the world, or is the world affecting us? Love not the world then, but SAVE it. 2 Peter 3:10 tells us where the WORLD is physically headed. It will be "dissolved." Consider that a prophetic fact! Why be excited about something that will end up being nothing? Why gamble on a slot machine in Vegas, when you can lay that $10 in an offering plate?

A lot is said today about church music, dress, and social activities. A guiding scripture was written to the Corinthians. (1 Corinthians 10:31)"Whatever you do, do all to the Glory of God." That's a constant challenge! How do you dance or sing? We've gone from beautiful organ music written by Bach and Beethoven to rockabilly written by anyone. Songs that now say, "God is great, God is good, rah, rah God." I can't wait for Revelation 4, when I'm singing with family and friends in that glorious place with no sinful nature(s) anymore. Praise God!

So it's about faith and attitude, my friend. Just make sure your modernization in fellowship is meant to GLORIFY our Savior. Don't bring the world system in as an attraction to the unsaved. But also, don't hang on to horses and buggies because change quenches your Spirit. It may just be your human nature either way.

JUST GLORIFY GOD!

COURAGE FOR MINISTRY 2021

I spent the entire weekend dealing with the subject of ministry in our modern age in America. For years, I've studied the advance of the "isms" of the world, while enjoying the freedoms created in my country via Christian Capitalism. This politic is based originally in Biblical texts such as Romans 13; with the full or partial realization that God (the Creator of everything) has supported free enterprise, and personal freedom. In our country, we pledge, at present, to be "one nation under God"...." with liberty and justice for all."

Now some have, over the years, not appreciated the true meaning of that freedom, and through power and politics, kept that potential from the weakest in our land. So we continue to fight for the freedom of all to this day. We have now entered something new in this time, referred to as the WOKE period. Essentially it is the "Godless" approach to life, looking for the ones in this culture who are to blame for all our societal ills.

To stand up to WOKE-ism, our guest speaker suggested we appropriate the courage of David as outlined in 1 Samuel: 16, 17. Have you killed a bear with your bare hands lately? How about wrestling a lion? This David guy was no pansy. It should not surprise anyone that after years of perfect practice, he saw himself downing Goliath, the 9-foot behemoth, with a slingshot. On top of that, David claimed in 17: 47, "the battle is the Lord's."

I'm sadly reporting as we enter the 2020's that we are under attack as Christians. In worldwide countries, Christians are being killed for their faith in their homes, businesses, and even their churches. In the comfortable confines of USA suburbs, we are seeing initial interfaces with school boards, politicians, and social groups. God is out again, and it isn't pretty. It takes a lot of "courage" to object to evolution, abortion, trans-genderism, etc., and it might just cost you your business, your job, or, yes, your freedom.

Our pastor taught from John 1 this evening, and spoke of Christ's ministry and courage. In picking disciples, He called one of them the "rock," knowing of Peter's future and not his present. It took years of teaching, training, observation, and struggle for Peter to develop into that rock, but he made it, only to die in the most humiliating fashion at the end.

So what's your bear look like? Are you ready to wrestle? Will you die for your flock?

What is your ministry? How are you gifted? Have you been training?

Just remember, as David did,

"The battle is the Lord's"

CREATION and CREATORS   2021

Until the mid-1800s, citizens of the USA were taught and accepted the idea they were created by God and their parents. A man named Darwin came along and changed all that! An option for non-believers was the premise that life is by accident and evolution. We began "becoming" some billion's of years ago in a primordial soup, and progressed to our current state through evolution until a few apes got brains and morphed into us.

This whole evolution trip began as some homo sapiens rejected the Bible (Word of God), saying there was no need for a Creator God (Genesis 1:1) and had to come up with some creative theory for our existence. If God is real, gave us His Word, and the Word became flesh, then the rejection of that as history will be deadly in the short run and the long run. In point of His Word, "the wages of sin is death."

If our creation then is both personal and universal, how should we react? We have two considerations, I submit, our God and our parents. We live in a culture which has tilted to the side today of neither. I also submit that the rejection of parents is no more than a rejection of God. It's so important to God that it's the 5th of the TEN Commandments. God loves us and hopes that we will always hold to honoring our parents. But the opposite is a very slippery slide, especially when one leaves their parentage to join another in marriage and raise a family. Loyalties do shift, and that's scriptural, Genesis 2. But it doesn't have to be at the expense of honor toward your Creator/creators.

In Colossians 3:23, we read: " whatever you do, work at it with all your heart, as working for the Lord, not for men, since you know that you will receive an inheritance." In our material society, it's incredibly easy to focus on these 60-80 yrs, leaving God, and maybe parents, out of the picture. As I write this brief, the 3 richest men in our society are taking trips to outer space. Amazing accomplishments, I think. Yet not one of them has acknowledged our Creator and His creation (Romans1). Our country's founders did! In fact, they credit our Creator with the gifts of life, liberty, and the pursuit of happiness.

So, where do you stand today? Are you an appreciative, created being? Or are you the master of your own destiny who has evolved to the supreme position of self-reliance, no longer recognizing the substantial gifts others have given you in your life or the Creator of your life?

I've been reading a small book on service of recent. A poignant sentence caught my attention. "There is no more perfect example of self-giving service than the ONE who left heaven when He could have stayed, and who stayed on the CROSS when He could have left." Do you appreciate your creation? Do you appreciate all those involved in that creation process? Could you be more thankful if you attended to those facts, seeing Christ in your life and future GLORY because of all those involved?

Enjoy your life! It is a gift. Be thankful for all those in your creation process. The return in riches, of all sorts, is substantial. ☺

DEATH #1 DEALING WITH IT BIBLICALLY 2021

I think this topic is the "elephant in the room" in most people's lives. We get encouragement as Christians, when Paul states, "to live is Christ, and to die is gain." (Philippeans1: 21). Even in the O.T., we see "God reserves wrath for His enemies." (Nahum 1: 2), and further," The Lord is good…And He knows those who take refuge in Him." (Nahum 1:7). He ends the entire Bible in Revelation 21 & 22 by giving us a picture of the Heavenly abode for those who place their trust in their Creator in this life. Sadly, He describes the alternative in Revelation 19 & 20 for those who reject of their own choice.

I've had death brought up thrice this past week. Firstly, a neighborhood friend died surprisingly. No, it wasn't Coved 19, a mosquito bit him, and the disease was encephalitis. It seemed so sad for this ex-wrestler in good physical condition, who loved the Lord, and it was quite untimely. Secondly, a friend asked for an explanation concerning what the Bible says about the second death. Thirdly, the subject arose about the topic as it is envisioned by the well-known offshoots of Christianity (cults) that can't accept the obvious presentations of death in the Bible.

The Bible speaks of eternal life in john 3, and covers quite well who is "saved" and who is condemned. In Romans 6:23, we see the "wages of sin is death, but the free gift of God is eternal life in Christ Jesus our Lord." So death is a mandate that we earn through life if you've been born. What happens then? That's where the arguments and speculation begin. Millions of people avoid scripture and take off in their own directions, following preachers who make up personal conclusions, and I propose, take a few of the masses with them. So what does the Bible actually say about all this death stuff?

As quoted earlier, you will earn your wages. You will be boxed up and buried or cremated. Then what? In Hebrews 9: 27, we read: "and inasmuch as it is appointed for men to die ONCE, and after this comes judgment." That's pretty clear to me. And you? In Daniel 12: we read, "and many of those who sleep in the dust of the ground, will awake, these to everlasting life, but the others to disgrace and everlasting contempt." So much for soul sleep! I wanna be in that everlasting group, how about you?

In Revelation 20: 14-15, it speaks of the "lake of fire" and the second death. As a human, we see that you die once, but the second transition is to eternal life in glory or to the lake of fire. Both are apparently eternal, according to scripture. That's both glorious and tragic. The avenue for glory is to be written in the Lamb's book of life. We read in verse 15: "If anyone's name was not found written in the book of life, he/she was thrown into the lake of fire."

You just read that. It's scripture! Please believe it.

I did. ☺

DEATH #2 THE JESUS VACATION   2021

I finished #1 a couple of days ago and then heard a message from Pastor Chuck out of Ecclesiastes on the topic. He presented it in total empathy as he shared the fact he suffered from a disease called Lupus. Modern technology brings comfort to the suffering, as discipline, medicine, and diet help to arrest what would have been deadly in Solomon's time. Nonetheless, this gray cloud hangs over his life as he thinks of his immediate family and their loss if he passes.

I mentioned the loss of a friend where I live in my other brief on the subject. There are just some passing's that aren't planned for, anticipated, or expected. But death is a mandate, like it or not. Ecclesiastes 9 is taught to be one of the Bible's most negative chapters, as Solomon laments the antithesis of birth. Chapter9:5 states, "For the living know that they will die." It seems strange that people, in general, consider, insure for, and plan for death but give little serious time to their potential destination.

Giving precedent to life, Solomon states in verse 4, "even a live dog is better than a dead lion." Dogs were way down the totem pole then. He also exhorts in verse 7:" Go, eat your food with gladness, and drink your wine with a joyful heart for it is now that God favors what you do." In other words, enjoy the life you've been given.

I have found that most people struggle in life because they have no blessed idea where they are going when they die. I came to realize in this last decade I've lived that: "the best is yet to come." With that realization in place with hope (Rev 21, 22), the rest of this life's existence for me has become significantly more important and fulfilling. Even my marriage has become more significant as Solomon subscribes: "Enjoy life with your wife" (Ecclesiastes 9)

The New Testament message is most encouraging, then. If you realize you have a Creator, accept His Love, and place your trust in Him, the future is bright. Ever look forward to a vacation? It's fun to anticipate and plan, but a little disappointing when it's over in a week. Well, the Jesus vacation is for eternity, And......it's better than anyone you've been on here. I've vaca'd from Miami to Honolulu, from San Tropes to Paris; and from Cancun to St Thomas. None of them have an edge on heaven, according to the Bible descriptions/brochures.

In Roman's 8: 18, Paul states: "I consider that our present sufferings (vacations) are not worth comparing with the GLORY that will be revealed...." And he finishes in 1 Corinthian 15, saying: "this mortal will have put on immortality," and "O death, where is your victory? Oh death, where is your sting"?

Have you applied your death repellant? Get sprayed today! ☺

DIAMOND OR ZIRCON! THE REAL THING
2021

For ten years, my wife Pat had the enjoyment of being employed by Tiffany and Company. For half that time, she handled the bridal registry. She had fun speaking with and serving more than a few well-known TV, movie, and business stars as they wished to obtain the very best for friends and loved ones. In the process, more than a casual acquaintance was developed for the beautiful crystal, necklaces, rings, and, of course, DIAMONDS.

One item never available at Pat's site was zircon stones. A zircon stone looks like a diamond, has facets like one, and is a bit brighter, but under the jeweler's scrutiny is anything but the real thing. Our diamond is the WORD (Bible). The first verse in the entire book defines God. Genesis 1:1 says He is the Creator of the world and Universe. After the first verse, the Bible, in its entirety, goes detail by detail about how God begins, continues, and ends, working with His creation. As the Pastors and teachers communicate the height and breadth of this classic work, it has outsold any other book in existence.

They are symbolically chipping facets from over this hardened "Word of God." The more facets that are chiseled, the brighter the ROCK becomes. Do you comprehend the visual? Our Rock: Jesus Christ is the basis for the facets. The more facets cut, the more amazing beauty brightens. Eventually, we reach the outrageous scene John describes in Revelation 4. There's an incredible song published today: "I can only Imagine," where a young man(Bart Millard) sees ahead to the day that He and his father will meet and love each other in heaven after many youthful years of abuse before conversion.

The zircon, then, isn't a diamond. This artificial diamond-looking substance has about a third the value because it's a fake. Over the years since its Creation, many fakes have arisen. False worship of golden calves, or the sun, or a distant untouchable god today worshipped by 1 ½ billion people, have always been created by people who have chosen to create their own gods to satisfy a longing for "something out there." Paul speaks on the subject in Acts 17:22+.

So what is the diamond of the world? Colossians 3:16 communicates the Biblical reality that Jesus the Christ is also Jesus the Creator. The Creator also communicated His Word to us. In that Word, He gave us the PAST Gen 1-3, the PRESENT John 1-3, and the FUTURE Rev 19-22. Every other hypothesis (zircons) is an attempt to negate scripture (the Creator's Word). The ultimate zircon replica will be the man, anti-Christ. This is because the pre-described diamond is the ROCK Himself, Jesus Christ.

The non-believers in today's creation aren't wearing a diamond. They look around for some kind of fake to substitute for the real thing. It may be a person, money, fame, or power. They believe in anything but the truth. What rock can they acquire, or wear as a substitute for the real thing? For a diamond to form, there must be pressure. Our pressure is the Ten Commandments. If you break them, you pay in eternity. If you accept the pressure and say you're sorry (repent), you've created the diamond.

"Seek you first His kingdom and righteousness, and all the rest will be added" Matthew 6:33.

DIFFERENCES, THEY MAY BE GOOD 2021

Do you think like me? Is that OK? "So what's the difference"? I read a book with that title 5 decades ago, and it's still a good read and contemporary. The point is, what's the truth about God, life, the Bible, and faith? Whom should I believe?

A plumb line is used by engineers to scope out distances and levels for construction when building. Fritz Ridenour used the term to define what truth in religion/Christianity really was/is. The Biblical plumb line is the gospel as defined by Paul in 1 Corinthians 15 that Christ died, was buried 3 days (a Jewish mandate to prove death), and resurrected and walked with His followers for 40 days. Some people who label themselves as Christians turn that around in various and sundry ways. They also redefine who Jesus Christ (the only begotten Son of God) is.

Over 80% of the earthly population denies God (the Creator) exists, and creates existential idols to worship. In other words, variety runs supreme, or maybe amuck. I use a weak analogy of ice cream to define positions of faith to flavors of ice cream. If you don't have the plain vanilla brand (the gospel), then you don't have ice cream. But after that, you have many different flavors. One famous American ice cream brand provides 31 different flavors. Whether rocky road ice cream or German chocolate cake, you are the same basic substance with a different flavor.

Using that analogy further then, we have many different flavors of Christians. Can vanilla say butter pecan isn't ice cream? Can strawberry cheesecake say chocolate isn't ice cream? Get the point? Paul used another analogy of the body in Romans 12 and 1Corintians 12. Can the eye say the feet are unnecessary? Or can the arm say the ear isn't needed? The basics are critical, but we see more denominations today than we do flavors. Christ said that if your hand offends you to cut it off, and we do indeed need to ferret out false theology and expunge it. So what of false opinions or applications by true believers?

I sometimes think that highly educated and pedigreed individuals forget they are studying and arguing over scriptures written by fishermen, sheepherders, and farmers. No discounting here for the work of the Holy Spirit, but that holds true for the professor and his salvation perspective, as well as the fisherman. When a person goes for a walk, can they discount the need for their arms? When one is in total darkness, can they discount the need for eyes at that point? Later on, those other body parts will be needed. So just as in life, we tend to make evaluations as we do in business. A company needs a good president, but he won't last too long running the place without secretaries, janitors, or delivery people.

We have Jesus Christ and the Bible. After that, we have Apostles, Prophets, Pastors, and Teachers (Ephesians 5) to give us, shepherd us, teach us, and lead us to God's Word. Just like the old game of passing a secret down a line of people, sometimes the messages get a bit garbled or misstated. That's when we go back to the original (the Gospel) and start over. Catholic and protestant application theology is quite different. But when a catholic "crosses" theirself, we realize we are sharing the same gospel. It's just that at the ends of the line, the Father, Son, and Holy Spirit can become quite different in application to life.

So keep your eyes on the "real" truth in Scripture. Are you really ingesting ice cream, or is it a pretend substance? Are you criticizing one another because they are just another flavor or body part? As a human, it's a challenge for the best of us. And the best process is to press forward in the Spirit of (Agape) LOVE.

ECCLESIASTES FIGHTING VANITY   2021

In Ecclesiastes 2: 11, the preacher states, "I considered all my activities which my hands had done and the labor which I had exerted, and behold all was vanity and striving after wind, and there was no profit under the sun." Take "under the sun" to heart, dear reader; it is mentioned multiple times to describe our station of existence in this life. This is a key, as all lives end in death. No escape; it reaches us all.

In verse 24, then, he states, "This also I have seen, that it is from the hand of God." In chapter 7: 14, the preacher states, "In the day of prosperity be happy. But in the day of adversity consider—God has made the one as well as the other." Do you get the picture? The Creator of the Universe is also active in our created lives. Keep in mind this 2nd chapter describes the life of he, who was David's son, and the King of Israel. His personal life was an abomination of riches, personal pleasure, and drunkenness.

The point then, to me, was that the attitude toward personal gain, pleasure, or material success was the vanity of vanities. Seeing everything as a gift from the hand of God gave those things meaning. Seeing any achievement in this life as based on individual godless activity is vanity. As my wife took note in service: "Meaning in (or to) life is given (by God), not gained."

Does this expunge personal initiative? I think not! But if one makes straight A's in school when they have been gifted with a 180-degree IQ, think about it. When one wins gold in the Olympics, with a body created thin and muscular, can they not be thankful for the gifted body they were given with which to train for excellence?

I think you can now see Solomon's conclusion. He gained the whole world (in his day) but was given his soul (by God). We need this lesson in "our" lives. Our country has lost it. One must ask where the Declaration today is, "We are endowed by our Creator with life, liberty, and the pursuit of happiness"? When we shift in allegiance from God to Government, haven't we created the politics of vanity? With God, we have the Ten Commandments. With government, we have excessive spending, immoral power grabs, and the murder of the unborn. Do you get it?

It's all in chapter 2, as shared. Is meaning in life "gifted" or "gained"? In his final analysis, the preacher went with gifted. How about you? Work hard and hone your giftedness. Maximize your talents in this world, but "GIVE GOD THE GLORY."

ECCLESIASTIES #2 SEEKING GOD'S PLAN
2021

To further benefit from this book and Solomon's life-learned experiences, we move forward to chapter 4. Remember that this man became the richest in history with unbridled satisfaction in material wealth and relational indulgences. And yet, in chapter 2:24, he concludes," A man can do nothing better than to eat and drink or find satisfaction in his work. This, too, I see, is FROM THE HAND OF GOD, for without Him, who can eat or find enjoyment"? "To the man who pleases Him, God gives wisdom, knowledge, and happiness, but to the sinner, he gives the task of gathering and storing up wealth to hand it over to the one who pleases God."

Setting the stage then, he travels through life's experiences which I have also seen as my latter days approach. There is a time for this and a time for that. It's an interesting and all accompanying list depicting one's lifetime. It starts with birth and ends with death. Chapter 3 sums up in verse 14, "God does it so that men will revere Him." In Exodus 20: 20, Moses is quoted, "Do not be afraid. God has come to test you so that the FEAR OF GOD WILL BE WITH YOU TO KEEP YOU FROM SINNING."

You should be getting the message by now. Solomon lived a life of total aggrandizement to show us the futility of material gain as opposed to a life of submission and appreciation to our Creator. Life is like a puff of smoke that he calls vanity. It passes like a vapor as it experiences the stages listed in Chapter 3. He notes that eventually, in verse 17, "God will bring to judgment, both the righteous and the wicked." So why do we live as if it will never end?

Where I live, the average age is over 80. Out of 2000 people, about 80 of them consider where they will be when they die. At present, they all worry about COVID-19, along with the consequences of it killing them. The 80 go to church hoping to find their eternal destiny. Most young people are more worried about success in this life (vanity), and could care less about eternity. I've been there and done that, as they say.

So the foundational theme of Ecclesiastes then is to focus on God's plan for your life (Jeremiah 29:11). "For I know the plans I have for you, declares the Lord." If you want to see the picture without God, read all the "stuff" about vanity. Everything in life is meaningless without God's guidance. I hope you're reading this at an early age. I wish I'd read and learned it in my 20's.

So I hope this leads the reader to keep the horse before the cart. It took Solomon and me an entire lifetime, and I'm still weeding out that which is meaningless and vanity. Don't let educators talk you out of your Creator. Don't let the wrong friends party you into meaninglessness. Learn the "fear of the Lord" in your life and "God's personal plan for you." Then go succeed, enjoy life, and make friends.

Solomon didn't use the word GRACE. Its use is prolific in the New Testament. But that's what he's talking about. One brief definition is being able to understand our Creator and what life is all about. If you receive it (GRACE), you will understand what life is all about and all the "times" in chapter 3. If you don't receive it, look forward to a meaningless life, full of vanity, passing like a vapor, no matter how much fun or successful. ☺

END TIMES: PROPHECY 2021

When one speaks of prophecy today, common thoughts lead to the future. In actuality, prophecy is any communication with God that mankind needs to hear. In fact, then, it covers the past, present, and future. In my Bible studies over the years, I use the dictum that one must process from the known to the unknown. One must process from the believable to the unbelievable. Using this didactical method, the reality of the unknown becomes the certainty of the known.

Therefore, Biblical history is written for the past, the present, and for the future. How can you believe that Christ will return if you don't believe He came in the first place? So we see that God created the world (Genesis 1:1), God came into the world (John 1), and God (Christ) will return to this planet (Zachariah 14, Acts 1). IT'S ALL PROPHECY, MY FRIEND.

As the Bible is historically accurate in the past, it is also then historically accurate for the future. I have written 2 briefs for this trilogy of end times which address some of the details about the future. As some predicted events have already transpired, beginning with the return of the Jewish nation to Israel, we can now see prophecy unfurl as a flag, with details listed in Ezekiel, Daniel, Zachariah, the Gospels, Thessalonians, and of course, Revelation at the end of scripture.

Don't worry that Christians have varying interpretations, perspectives, time frames, or deductions. The common thread of God's salvation for some, and judgment for others, is mainstream. The common thread of Christ's return, at some point, is mandated. The need for repentance, forgiveness, and restoration in Christ is uniform. Stay focused on the "has to be's," and love one another on the details of our future.

God has prophesied what He wishes us to know. Sometimes it's confusing. That's why we have so many denominations within the Christian faith. And yet, He did take the time to share the wealth on creation, sustaining, and looking forward to the promised payoff for eternity. I covered all this in my brief on studying the Bible.

So delve in, my reader. Learn the history of life. Learn how to please your Creator in this life, and certainly, enjoy learning God's plans for the future as you grow in the faith.

Enjoy the trip! It's a blast. ☺

END TIMES: TRAINING FOR THE TRIBULATION 2021

The Bible speaks of one last 7-year period, prophesized in the book of Daniel, chapter 9. God has revealed, if you know where to look, certain events for the future at varying times in the past. He covers the necessity of judgement from time to time, based on mankind's rejection of His love and forgiveness. FORGIVENESS? For what do you ask? Broke one of the 10 commandments lately? Society, in general, has proven to ignore, defy, or just plain be ignorant of its Creator. At some point, the Creator responds.

God responded in Noah's day, Sodom's/Lots day, and Israel's/Babylon's day. The Bible now predicts an upcoming day. Why do I say upcoming? Ezekiel 34 begins the final scenario of the return of the Jews to Israel. It happened in my lifetime with the reforming of the State of Israel in 1948. I have likened this in the past to the Indians retaking Manhattan Island.

Nothing in history seems to happen on an overnight basis. It's much like the frog being boiled in water. Throw it in boiling water, and it will immediately jump out. Place it in cool water, brought to a boil, and it will slowly be cooked and die. I've lived in that cool water for decades now, but the temperature is rising. It seems obvious to be headed for the boiling point. That boiling point will take place in the final week of Daniels's 70 weeks (of years), called the great tribulation.

I believe as I pen this "1-page brief" that the time has arrived. It all began with Israel's rebirth. It now continues with items too parallel to scripture to be a coincidence. We are in a significant pandemic at present. Mankind says to be shot with a vaccine, and millions/billions of people are taking it and "demanding" all others comply. This isn't the tribulation, and the vaccine isn't the mark of the beast, but society has no problem with this training, to line up en masse and be "saved."

How about money for buying and selling? (Revelation 13) The latest version is called bit-coin. This currency is digital and fully able to be controlled by the central powers. Without it, you will be broke in the purest sense. How about distribution? Our markets depend on overseas shipments to ports of entry. Revelation 18:17 speaks of sea captains, in my version, lamenting the fall of the Babylon system, as they can't unload their goods for purchase.

Have you seen the news on shipping to California at present? We're not in the tribulation yet, so it must be a training exercise.

And lastly, how about wars or rumors of the same, or famines or earthquakes or fires that Christ spoke about in Matthew 24:1-14. Have you watched the news lately? Has California been burning? Have you heard about the shaking around the Pacific Rim, or the San Andreas Fault? Did you know that 25,000 people die of starvation each DAY? I believe we're well into the training season, folks.

And so, dear reader, I exhort you. Take your training period seriously. Let your un-repentant friends know what this is all about. It's just about game day. Store some oil up for your lamp. (Matthew 25:1-13)All the signs are in place; we just don't know the game time!

END TIMES: FOR PLANET EARTH 2020

It all began in 1970. I attended evening church taught by a 30 yr old Dr John MacArthur and a Bible study at UCLA led by a 30yr old Hal Lindsey. I was hooked. I learned God (the Creator) was as active and specific about the future as He was about history; the past. Given that, I began to notice how perfectly accurate the Bible is, God's Word (John 1). Based on that premise, I then began to study what His Word had to say about the future.

For the purpose of this writing, I will isolate 4 or 5 items of certainty that Christians can therefore take to the bank.

1) The Messiah came and was killed in perfect timing, as predicted in the book of Daniel. (Daniel 9: 24-26)

2) As the disciples walked to Jerusalem for Passover, Jesus told them he would be captured, flogged, and killed by the authorities (Mark 8:27-33), BUT would come back to bodily life in 3 days. Need I say more? They didn't get it until Pentecost, when the Holy Spirit filled them and opened their eyes.

3) Israel has been reborn. The Jewish people have returned. The Bible predicted this event in numerous places for the time of the end. It has happened. You might read Ezekiel beginning with Chapter 36 to the end of the book. This is akin to Indians moving back in and reclaiming NYC's Manhattan Island. Israel is surrounded by 1.5 BB Muslims. Are today's Israeli Jews a modern-day Gideon's army???

5)   1st Thessalonians 4 predicts a time when all believing, born-again Christians will be removed from the earth in a "beam me up Jesus" event referred to as the "Rapture" or taking away. That's how the Bible describes Jesus Christ's exit from the earth in Acts 1.

6) In Rev 11, 2 key witnesses will preach the gospel in Jerusalem, be killed, and rise again in 3 days, as the whole world watches. In Revelation 13, God shares that we won't be able to buy and sell without having an official number. Do you have any credit cards or SS numbers? We take technology for granted today as we see live action around the world as it takes place, but scripture was written over 2000 years ago.

There is a great deal more to study and review. In 1 Thessalonians 4, Christ returns in the clouds. In Zachariah 14, His feet touch the Mount of Olives, and the mountain splits, and water gushes forth. These are, very obviously, to be two different events. Detail to follow. Suffice it to say that we are living in a most exciting time. As born-again Christians, we've been shown the details of these events and can appreciate the veracity of Scripture

It's great to realize God is still in control. He created this world. Get it? He controls this world, including the weather. Get it? He controlled the past, and He will control the future. I hope you get it!!! ☺

END TIMES: REBUILDING THE TEMPLE OF GOD IN JERUSALEM 2021 (October, 2014)

Let's turn to Ezekiel.

A _**TIMELINE**_ was set up 2500+ years ago in this prophecy. It kicks off in chaps 36 & 37 with the Jewish nation returning to Israel. This happened in the last century and solidified with the nation forming legally in 1948. In Chap 38, we see the countries of the middle east responding. The countries surrounding Israel are listed, such as Iran, Ethiopia, Libya, Turkey etc., with their former names. The land of Gog/Magog is listed, and it's speculated to be Russia (and/or maybe Turkey). Continuing, we see the great attack from the North that God stops "alone" with a great earthquake. Starting in Chapter 40 then, the 3rd temple is described, measured, located, and set up for Jehovah/Christ's reign on earth.

The concern then is where the new Temple will be built. In Chapter 38, this destructive earthquake is so severe that in verses 19 and 20, we are told that in Israel, **"every wall will fall to the ground."** Who cares about the Dome of the rock, the Temple Mount, or the City of David? They are toast. They're leveled. If you jump forward to Zachariah 14, you will discover that God will return later, and a giant split in the Mount of Olives will occur. This will form an explosion of water such that the flow down the hill to the Dead Sea will be so great that this Dead Sea will come to life for freshwater fishing from the shore. (Ezekiel 47). That's the 1st place I went on my visit to Israel.

One can therefore see the land leveled at the beginning of Daniel's final 7-year period (Daniel 9:26, 27). Everything in Israel is leveled, including Jerusalem and the Dome of the Rock, and the City of David. Ezekiel 39:9 says it will take the Israelis "7" years to clean up the mess from all the dead ground troops. I personally believe the ground attack bolsters the event of the "Rapture" occurring beforehand to remove all current Christians from the earth's surface, thus opening the door for the Russians, Iranians, and maybe Turks to attack.

In this brief study, one must read the above noted Bible references, which will allay any concern for the location of the next Temple for Christ's reign.

It's at Jerusalem, built on the new topography, unaffected by Jehovah's (Christ's) return and the splitting in two of the Mount of Olives with a new river flowing out from below the Temple (Ezekiel 47).

This scenario fits comfortably with current news headlines: 1) Israel is in place; (1948) 2) The countries around it are crumbling; (2014-21) 3) The Christians of this world are beginning to take a back seat. (Abortions and same-sex marriage 2014-21) 4) we have reached the point that all remaining people could be forced to buy and sell with prescribed numbers and IDs. The memory center is being constructed in southern Utah (2014). 5) The whole world is looking for ***strong leadership,*** which will emerge after the destruction of Russia, Turkish, Syrian and Iran's armies by God. There will be a great and powerful world leader, who at the halfway point of the 7 years, will take a place in the newly constructed Temple and demand the people's worship. **The stage has been set.**

LUKE 21:28: BUT WHEN THESE THINGS BEGIN TO TAKE PLACE, STRAIGHTEN UP AND LIFT YOUR HEADS, BECAUSE YOUR REDEMPTION IS DRAWING NEAR

END TIMES: The Final Pieces of the Puzzle
2021

As we have shared over the past few years, events have shaped the world scene such that one can conclude that, as God predicted for us, the end of this age is upon us. In sharing from both the Old and New Testaments, we can now watch as if in a motion picture:

Israel! Its rebirth is essential and mandated by Ezekiel 35 forward. It's absolutely miraculous (God involved) that the Jews have returned and re-incorporated this State of Judaism. As the chapters proceed, we see the countries surrounding Israel are conflicted but in strenuous opposition to the rebirth of this tiny nation, and the entire world of 2021 is against it. In continuing, wars will take place, the Temple will be constructed, the topography will change, and waters will pour forth from the Temple Mount.

Zachariah 14:

In this chapter, we see the return of Christ. It states that He will come to earth and land on Mt Moriah. At that point, a giant earthquake will result, and waters will gush forth to the East. These waters are described in detail in the Ezekiel section with varying levels of depth until the flows reach the Dead Sea, which will become fresh enough to become a fishing locale.

Daniel 9

In Daniel 9, we see a timeline, demanding a final period of 7 years to fulfill the prophecy. This period of timelines is up well with what is called a great tribulation. God has "never" allowed sin and rebellion to proceed on earth unpunished. This tribulation period has been set apart for the final time for people to repent. If they do, all is forgiven. If they don't, they will die and be rewarded for their choice. Revelation shows that half or more of the world's population will be taken out during this brief period of judgment.

Matthew 24

Christ speaks of and describes a period of time in which no one wants to live. In His zeal for personal salvation, He nonetheless shares that many will reject the Creator's free gift of love, and suffer the punishment. It is a nasty experience ending in the greatest war ever known to mankind. Revelation 19 speaks of the Valley of Meggeddon, where the worst conflagration in world history will take place. Millions will die, and the blood will rise to the horse's bridles. Then, Christ will return.

Revelation 20

This entire chapter focuses on Christ ruling this earth from the city of Jerusalem. This is mentioned earlier in Ezekiel as only the Spirit of the Lord can enter the East gate of Jerusalem. Christ will rule fairly and justly, yet some will still not believe. Those who do will be blessed, and those who don't; won't. This period of time will encompass 1000 years. So the earth we know is going nowhere for the present

1st and 2nd Thessalonians

An event must take place which seems imminent but can't be determined exactly. All believers will be meeting Christ in the air for a glorious reunion. This has been labeled today as the "rapture" It appears as different from Zachariah 14, when Christ lands with His feet, in Jerusalem on Mt Moriah. It will be an amazing event and totally change the world system dynamic, as all existing "born again" Christians will be taken away. It makes great human sense that the forces of evil and world powers will feel free at this point to attack Israel without resistance, only to be stopped by God with a giant earthquake, as noted in Ezekiel 38. The death and destruction are so great it will take 7 years to clean it all up.

That's the biblical future, dear friend. Read it and rejoice, or read it and weep!

The Final Pieces of the Puzzle (Events that must happen, that haven't as of 2021)

>As we have shared over the past few years, events have shaped the world scene such that one can conclude that what God predicted for us, the end of this age, is upon us.

So let's get right to it:

>Israel! Its rebirth is essential and mandated by Ezekiel 35 forward. It's absolutely miraculous (God involved) that the Jews have returned (9MM in Israel) and re-incorporated this State of Judaism. As the chapters proceed, we see the countries surrounding Israel are in conflict and in strenuous opposition to the rebirth of this tiny nation, and the entire world of today is against it.

Study, or at least read these chapters slowly, and you will swear you are following the news reports of today:

>1st and 2nd Thessalonians

An event must take place which seems imminent but can't be determined exactly. All believers will be meeting Christ in the clouds for a glorious reunion. This has been labeled today as the "rapture." It appears different from Zachariah 14, when YHWAH/CHRIST lands with His feet, in Jerusalem on Mt Moriah. After the "rapture," It makes great human sense that the forces of evil and world powers will feel free at this point to attack Israel without resistance, only to be stopped by God with a giant earthquake, as noted in Ezekiel 38. The death and destruction are so great it will take 7 years to clean it all up.

>Zachariah 14:

In this chapter, we see the return of Christ. It states that He will come to earth and land on Mt Moriah. At that point, a giant earthquake will result, and waters will gush forth to the East. These waters are described in detail in the Ezekiel section with varying levels of depth until the flows reach the Dead Sea, which will become fresh enough to become a fishing locale.

>Daniel 9

In Daniel 9, we see a timeline demanding a final period of 7 years to fulfill the prophecy. This period of timelines is up well with what is called a great tribulation. God has "never" allowed sin and rebellion to proceed on earth unpunished. This tribulation period has been set apart for the final time for people to repent. If they do, all is forgiven. If they don't, they will die and be rewarded for their choice. Revelation shows that HALF or more of the world's population will be taken out during this brief period of judgment.

>Matthew 24

Christ speaks of and describes a period of time in which no one wants to live. In His zeal for personal salvation, He nonetheless, shares that many will reject the Creator's free gift of love and suffer the punishment. It is a nasty experience ending in the greatest war ever known to mankind. Revelation 19 speaks of the Valley of Megiddo (I passed through on my visit to Israel), where the worst conflagration in world history will take place. Millions will die, and the blood will rise to the horse's bridles. Then, Christ will return.

>Revelation 20

This entire chapter focuses on Christ ruling this earth from the city of Jerusalem. This is mentioned earlier in Ezekiel. Only the Spirit of the Lord can enter the East gate of Jerusalem. Christ will rule fairly and justly, yet some will still not believe. Those who do will be blessed, and those who don't will not. This period of time will encompass 1000 years. So the earth we know is going nowhere for the present

Take heed, my friend. The end seems near. The ARK is almost finished, and God will shut the door. Alllllllll Aboarddddd!

EQUIPING THE SAINTS.... FOR WHAT?

2021

I read Ephesians 4 again, for the ??th time. It's a go-to passage for the description of church training and its purpose. Why do people go to Bible school? Why do Christian educators go to seminary? It's due to the need for focused, advanced, in-depth Biblical studies, for the sole purpose of teaching others "to equip the saints, for the "work" of the ministry." This is all handled by the churches through advanced studies in Theology, and aggressive fellowship in gatherings of small to larger groups so as to work out the attended ministries.

Most churches are relatively small, and there is little problem with people knowing one another. In modern times, however, (last 100 years), and with the advent of audiovisuals, we now see what are referred to as mega-churches. One can get good theology there, but also weak theology, usually dependent on the pastors' pedigree and training. Fellowship can be strong or weak, as well as ministry. It is quite common for fellowships to divide into multiple church gatherings, as opposed to having one large building and gathering.

So what's the purpose, then, according to Ephesians 4? The purpose is to equip the saints for the work of the ministry. How do you know this is happening? Very simply, people step forward with new ministries out of the fellowship. I saw Rick Warren recently sharing the goals of Saddleback Church in Ca, to "reach the world" with the GOSPEL. With that as a focus, there over 20,000 members have gone to over 190 countries with that in mind, heart, and soul. Not bad for starting in his family living room.

What hinders that and keeps churches from growing? I believe it to be a word I've coined, or created, called churchyness. It happens when well-equipped members come forward with new ministries, and are met with resistance by well-meaning (?) church leaders. Common reasons for resistance are: no rooms, no child care, or maybe you're not properly trained. Is that the example Jesus used as He picked the disciples?

We should always realize that good theology being taught enlivens the creative juices, and people will step forward with new ministries to which they have been led. These "equipped" saints might probably be led by the

69

Holy Spirit for needs in that fellowship. The church might consider them DEACONS just to ensure God's qualifications for servant leaders are met. That seems more profitable than snuffing out potential Spirit-led ministries for the wrong reasons.

Are parishioners coming forward as you grow? Find a room to make quilts, a room to Bible study share other than Sunday. Figure out ways to make buildings 7-day activity centers. A good church, theologically, will equip creative members, and they will come forward with new fellowship ministries.

MAKE WAY, and be awed by the results!

FAMILY #1: WHERE THE RUBBER MEETS THE ROAD 2021

My friend counsels people. One of the main topics is the family and the problems families face. If you don't, you're probably not breathing. Just so that you know, it's nothing new! As Scripture begins in Genesis 1-3, the man Adam is lonely. God creates a woman for him, she leads him astray as she is led astray, and he bites. A couple chapters later, they have two sons, and one murders the other. I'll spare you the details.

If the parents today don't mind what the kids are doing, they are probably living more in today's culture, and don't really care about God's Ten Commandments. We live in a society now where schools teach we evolved, as opposed to God creating everything. It's now OK to be active sexually, without marriage, if you create a life you don't want, just kill it, lie if it helps, steal if no one sees you, and of course, covet everything you don't have that your neighbor does. Lastly, don't honor your parents, which is right in the middle of the Ten. What's that doing in the midst of all those other constraints?

I meet each week to study and share the Scripture with a group of 12-15 men. Another 5-6 float through also. Not one of these men is without family issues. We share the woes, pray about them, search the scriptures for answers etc. In the first decade of one's life, children are a blessing. They begin to float in their teens and take it to the moon in their 20s. From there on, it's a crap shoot. The societal goal is material wealth. Get a job, get rich, and build an economic base for the future.

It may involve school; it may involve becoming an entrepreneur, or maybe just two hardworking kids who share an apartment or live at home to save or share expenses. At what point do we become masters of our own destiny? No need for a Creator, no need for parents, and totally grateful to ourselves for our abundance. We shared a birthday with friends recently, and she spoke of a dear college friend who had 4 daughters. The parents lavished them with a nice home, advanced education, and cars to boot. The girls don't like their parents anymore. The parents can't remember what they did to offend. Does it matter, as they may just be a target that was waiting to be hit?

In Matthew 12: 46-50, Jesus defines the family. His earthly family stood outside when He was speaking, and He was told about it. He didn't respond other than to say, "whoever does the will of the father in heaven is my brother and sister and mother." Do you have offspring or relatives in rebellion against their Creator just as you were at one time? If you can't "forgive as you were forgiven" (Colossians 3), it will show up in family relations. It's a process to work out that can only be changed by prayer and attitude.

Families have great decades and sad decades. One should never think the bad ones are permanent. One should also NEVER let the bad ones erase the good ones. Christ had a crucifixion for sure, but He also had a RESURRECTION 3 days later. He also spent another 40 days of real life with His disciples before shooting up into the clouds like a rocket (Acts 1). He will also return in the near future to meet His believers in the clouds (1 Thessalonians 4) and return to earth to land on His feet in Jerusalem (Zachariah 14).

I hope you get the picture that Scripture poses. There will be bad times with the creation of life in your earthly family. If you're on the outs with your kin, keep the faith. Stay strong with brothers and sisters in Christ. Hope and pray that Spirit is indeed "thicker than blood." You and your family will have much to gain in this short period of time we have here. Who knows? Maybe you will put my consular friend out of business. You will at least shorten his calendar ☺

FAMILY #2 LIFE PASSES ON 2021

This particular brief is motivated by the death and resurrection of my cousin Greg Miller. Greg had spent 77 years in a wheelchair cocooned by cerebral palsy. I have been writing these briefs, of late, on particular subjects regarding my Christian faith. The passing to eternity of my cousin of almost 8 decades made me ponder the sadness of one's passing, but also the JOY for one of my fellow BORN-AGAIN relatives.

The family tree all started at the beginning of the 20th century, in Paris, Ontario, Canada, where Grandma and grandpa Shafer were married. They planted the family tree in the Detroit area and raised the first 4 branches. From that seedling grew tens of offspring that settled in life from India to Boston to Arkansas, to Arizona, to Denver, and now even to Moscow, Idaho. What a trip??? ☺. The roots of this clan were planted in the Spirit of the Christian faith. No one exemplified that more than Cousin Greg.

Pat and I visited Greg twice after settling in Phoenix 8 years ago. It was a blessing to share with my cousin, who was a born-again man of faith (John 3). We talked and shared about normal things, but he enjoyed sharing his faith and especially how they drove him to services each week so he could worship his Creator. That's why, when I heard of Greg's passing, my heart/Spirit leaped with Joy for him. For those of us who experience the knowledge of Greg's trip through life, it hasn't been easy for him or the family.

BUT IT'S BEEN BLESSED!

Greg's legacy, then, is Greg's faith. The Shafer tree is now fully grown, in many directions, with many branches. My sister documented this well in a family album a few years ago. The branches are now numerous, as some have been pruned, and some just cut off (John 15). For those of you pruned, you will love my analogy. For those cut-off, you will probably be offended. Take it up with Jesus!

When Holly shared the news of Greg's passing, as stated, my heart leaped with JOY, as Greg emerged from his earthly cocoon, and transformed into a beautiful butterfly into the arms of Jesus. Praise God!

God knows and loves you! God knows and loves your kids. He wants you to Google him. Get on your Spiritual phone and start PRAYING. In Luke 8, the sick woman just touched His garment, after chasing Him, and was healed. Give the process some energy and effort as you see God work. Be patient, as God was with you. Want it because He wants it. Love them because He loves you. The results may be today, or way down the road.

Just don't give up! He didn't give up on you. ☺

FAMILY #4 RECEIVING RELATIVES AS STRANGERS 2021

We spent a weekend morning with a dear friend recently. She mentioned a child with whom she related most favorably and one she did not. Both are quite normal. Statistics bear this out as 30% of all marriages end in divorce, and 2/3 of children raised in Sunday school, no longer attend church. Why is everyone surprised? It's nothing new. (Hebrews 10:25) Cain murdered Abel, Ishmael hated Isaac, and Esau hated Jacob; nothing new!

God set up the program for marriage at the beginning of creation (Genesis2:24). Just fall in love and separate. This works well for the newlyweds but not always so well for the ones left. Parental ownership is not a hill to die on. To one degree or another, the newlywed will leave and "CLING" to the wife or husband. It's all classic and redundant.

I've been active in the Christian church for years, from coast to coast. I don't apologize, as it has been a source of great loving fellowship. At the same time, it has proven a family battleground for parents, children, and other relatives and acquaintances. I will guarantee that most of my good friends have processed through a divorce, and some have visited drug issues, and all have entertained rebellion. I'm on that list. WHY? We all have sinful natures, personalities that want to go against God's perfect plans for our lives.

Sin is a trickle-down process. We sin against God; from time to time. We work toward and hope to be forgiven and show up again. Our kids do the same thing. Eventually, those cute little rug rats will grow, mate, and create new little sin natures. The attendant goal, then, is to teach repentance, salvation, and glory. It's the process, my friend. The sadness is when it (salvation) happens to us and not to our children, friends, spouses, and neighbors.

Once saved, we learn about true prayer to our Savior. That's what really works. They no longer responded to your best wishes for them, just as you rejected God in the past. You have to give them time, as God gave you time. You are still a personage in their lives, but not necessarily an influence. To overcome this frustration, it seems that "we," the eldest, might recognize that the program in the family, changes.

I now look at my life in decades, and I've had 8. Some of these decades have really been great and fun and a blessing. Some have been tough, sad, and difficult. I personally grew in my Spiritual life during the tough ones. And I did enjoy the pleasant and happy ones as a human being. It's all a process, my friend, and I hope you're making the trip with God by your side. If any of your offspring take another trip, help them through, pray them through, but don't think you will control them through.

Our goal then for all relatives and acquaintances is: (1 Corinthians 2: 16). Share the God's loving gospel (1 COR 15). Help them to get saved, as we did, in body, mind, Spirit, and attitude. The process has never been, nor intended to be, easy in this life.

But the DESTINATION is worth the effort. ☺

FAMILY # 5 JOSEPHS SONS NAMING ONE'S CHILDREN 2021

I think the trials and tribulations of life are most exemplified in the personality of Joseph. He was actually a "good guy." However, the 1st 3 decades weren't all that easy for him (Genesis 37). The scripture evaluates that period by saying: "you meant evil against me, but God meant it for good." His brothers had sold him into slavery, having come to the point of disliking/hating him. Families are like that.

Falling away from the family tree has been going on since creation. One of the first 2 brothers murdered his sibling. Joseph's brothers literally sold him off because he was dad's favorite. Joseph was a powerful and bright man of faith. His prayer life and ability to interpret dreams led to his eventual leadership in Egypt; but not until he rotted in jail for 7 years.

So what's your family issue? Kids fighting, or you no longer can stomach your parents? 1/3 of all marriages end up in divorce today, and 90% of parents have family members who don't like them anymore.

So Joseph named his 2 sons Manasseh: "God has made me forget all my trouble," and Ephraim: "God has made me fruitful"(Genesis 41: 50-52). I'm sure that during their 1st decade, the family celebrated their creation and existence, as Joseph's life had certainly changed from disaster to prosperity. Is that the story of your existence or history? Did you have tough times and family issues? It seems to be endemic to living.

So what's my point in this "1-page brief"? Family, being part of, or creating one, is fantastic in its potential for joy. God did it when He created the family of man. But get ready dear reader. God's creation turned on Him and still does. I turned on mine for a time. You will turn on yours from period to period. One or some of your offspring, if you have any, will turn on you. The statistics bear me out.

Turn to God. Ask for forgiveness for yourself first. Ask for reconciliation next. Life isn't about being happy all the time or even getting along with all family, friends, or acquaintances. But Biblical life is indeed about being JOYFUL all the time. When you look at the lives of those who the Holy Spirit chose to write the New Testament, their lives were anything but happy. And their death processes were worse. But their JOY was in the Lord, and they exemplified it, believed it, and wrote about it.

If you study regularly in the Bible, you will find where we are today is, indeed, nothing new. How you resolve problems in this life, with God's help or without, seems to be your choice. I recommend the former, and positive experience can predict a better outcome.

Good luck doesn't seem appropriate to the author here. But God bless your Spirit and effort, does.

Enjoy the trip, I have! ☺

FAMILY # 6 LIFE IN DECADES 2021

I'm at the end of my 7th decade now, and the idea came to me recently due to a family disagreement. Ever have one? The thought crossed my mind that this disagreement could ruin history until I realized that history can be dated and segmented. WW11 was awful. It was a bad decade. The family of any given soldier who died was broken; forever. As their children grew up in the 50's and 60's, however, the decades were potentially wonderful.

As I thought of the consternation of my offspring, I thought of earlier points in my life that were both joyful and happy. Children, for example, can rebel at any age. They can be rebellious in the 1st decade, but mostly in the 2nd, and possibly later decades, over unhealed psychological wounds they can't or won't give up. I was late in losing my disobedience, but seemed to appreciate that my parents worked with the talents God gave them to the best of their abilities. I was able to give up the weight of rebellion later on and carry no burden of thought in the passing of my parents. When God said, "honor your father and mother," He had a reason. It's a challenging arena of rebellion for many.

I had great memories from my 1st decade, having spent most of it in Battle Creek, Mi. When I got a bike, I was free at last! ☺. My second decade was in Wichita, where I started slow but finished strong and with a smile. The 3rd recorded new experiences, new children, a new business, and all that is involved (pain and happiness).

I think here that the premise is simple. Bad decades don't erase good decades (unless you let them). Good decades don't erase bad ones. When in a good one, enjoy it. When in a bad one, live it to the full, as it may bless you later. You will learn as this proceeds I'm a man of faith; faith in the Creator of this world. Faith in Him who's Son gave me the promise of eternal decades; in a timeless universe (heaven). When He sacrificed Himself on the cross, it was His worst day. When He arose 3 days later, it was His best. In my life, I have had "cross" days and days of "rising." I've had decades of pain and decades of rising.

In this monolog of encouragement, I think of each of my decades and comment on those some of my relatives might be experiencing. You can relate to my experience and think of your own rich experiences. Maybe you were drunk for 10 years, or are! Maybe you ran from your family in one decade and formed a new one in another. If you've had 5-7 decades, you already know things can be good and otherwise......

To be sure, life can be great, and the opposite. I've been to Europe 10-12 times, cruised 6-8 times, and been to China, Israel, 50 states, and all but 3 State capitals. To me, that's been great and given me some great decades. I obviously enjoyed traveling. I lettered 6 times in football, but no all-conference. (One of my granddaughters was all-conference softball). I have about a year-extra over college and averaged A- in that. (Not as an undergraduate☹) All these activities came with an extracurricular effort, which at times gave me partial decade of frustration. And, I made a family!

So look back in years. Look forward to years. If you are blessed(?) with a long life, you can look backward in decades as I have. You will get some bad ones, but as stated, super-enjoy the good ones; I have!

If you are reading this little 7th decade expose' in book form, I MADE/DID IT!

FOCUS: BE ANXIOUS FOR NOTHING
(PHILIPPIANS 4: 4-9)   2021

As I contemplate the day, I find my mind filled with the frustrations of life, family, purpose, and the inability to focus on my God-given privileges. As per usual, in a moment of prayer, God's Spirit directs me to a passage as a quick and solid reminder of the mental and Spiritual path I need to take.

As I read and absorb my latest endeavor, which is the biography of Thomas Jefferson, I'm reminded that all who pass through this life deal with the same encounters of frustration as all those before. No great prophet, politician, leader, successful business icon, or pastor has gone without obstacles to overcome, from deprivation to death, to personal family, friends, or…

And so as I enjoy the fruit of life in solitude, with soft music in the background, that even David enjoyed personally, or for others, I am suddenly struck with the thought of the above Scripture. As Paul chides a couple of the local church b....es, and reminds the followers and saved to forbearance, he then segues into where we should focus.

As I contend with my spouse, take hurtful and untruthful jibes from my children, contemplate going back into the workaday fray, and ignore the prospect of a simple life available to me for relaxation, I see myself in a disgusting, unappreciative, and non-forbearing mood.

WHAT A WASTE!

On the other hand, it certainly proves the reality and conclusions of God's Word. It's real and all around us. The unregenerate wallow in activities and seek "that" which they will leave behind.

Could Solomon be more inspired and his Ecclesiastes more correct? Give me everything in this life, and I need, and I demand more. Give me nothing but to share, and I am at the "very least fulfilled."

And so again, I've been brought down, and the need to re-focus returns. I'm not always placed where I wish to be, but where I need to be. I need to re-list the 3 main items where I would be guided out of my or others; abyss. If you wallow, you become muddy. If you wrestle (with pigs); muddier.

FAMILY #3 CONFLICT REALITY 2021

When one has family conflict, they tend to hide the fact from others. When all is well, they hang a banner on the front of the house. The kids graduated from college. The kids got married and had grandkids. The kids got a promotion. Here's what you don't hear: the kid flunked out, the kid's shack-mate is pregnant, the kid had a divorce, or unfortunately, the kid had an abortion. That's the world of today.

Is it new? How about the kid who killed his brother (Cain)? How about the kid who had sex with her and killed her husband (David), or the kid who had 700 wives and 300 concubines (Solomon)? There is nothing new "under the sun" (Ecclesiastes). I was feeling bad as one of our children decided not to like us anymore. I then listened as all the 12-15 men that I share/Bible study with have unsaved kids or ones that just don't like their parents. I asked my counselor/pastor how many families had kids that didn't like them, and he said 90%. I read in a book that I was reading, "Have You Considered?," that "2/3 of children raised in Christian homes are now leaving church."

I'm not pointing a finger without realizing 3 are pointing back at me. In my youthful exuberance, after all that my parents had done for me, including a free college education, my wife and I eloped. I'll skip the details, but what a slap in the face to both sets of parents. The same God who created "In the Beginning" (Genesis 1) also said: "a man shall leave his father and his mother and hold fast to his wife, and they shall become one flesh." (Genisis2:24) He later stated in the 10 Commandments #5, "Honor your father and your mother" (Exodus 20:12). It's not either or, but rather both and.

So what's my attitude concerning family? What a blessing. Offspring are a joy, whether it's for 1, 2, or3 decades; maybe 5, 6, or 7. Have you experienced anything in life where you didn't have to take the bad with the good? It's just the program for the last 6000 years of recorded history. Have you tried prayer? Why don't you Google God? (see my brief on prayer). He's aware of your situation, you know. God protected Cain, and God elevated Joseph from the bloody pit of his brothers to kingship in Egypt and lovingly saved his family. He made David King, and God made his son Solomon wealthy, because David was his dad.

Oh God, save me! Oh Spirit, guide me. Oh mind, be renewed. Oh flesh, be the caboose of it all! We aren't exhorted to "joice," but to re-joice. We're not admonished to be anxious but to "be anxious for nothing." I love this beautiful set of reminders to the Philippians!

Go have yourself a day of excellence!   ☺

FORGIVE AS THE LORD FORGAVE YOU

2021

As this passage in Colossians 3 was shared in a message Sunday, it hit me like a brick. That's why I love to worship, attend church, study Bible, and write down my created thoughts as a result. At this point, the old hymn "Nearer my God to thee" has more meaning, and retirement gives me excess time to meditate and create without the rigors of schedule and work. It's a blessing!

Right before this statement on an attitude and actions of forgiveness, we are admonished to clothe ourselves in "compassion, kindness, humility, gentleness, and patience." I've done this over the years with people whom I like or love, but what about the others? Paul moves forward, saying "Bear with each other, and forgive whatever grievances you may have against one another." In other scriptures, we see, Love one another, Love your enemy, Honor your mother and father, etc.

And then I'm hit right between the eyes, as it's said. "Forgive as the Lord forgave you." Now I have really come to realize, at this point, just how much God has forgiven me. It only happened as a result of my being "Born Again," in the Spirit. Throughout my life, I've witnessed all these thoughts and actions of mine, which go against the standards God has set for perfection. The Jewish people were given over 600 rules and regulations, but we all know "the Big Ten." When Christ taught God's standards, He said to follow them and that even thinking about them was an act of action.

In the book of James, we read: "For whoever keeps the whole Law and yet stumbles at just one point is guilty of breaking all of it." So when, back in the day, I dishonored my parents from time to time, I was just as guilty before God as if I had committed adultery or murdered. In society, we have varying degrees of crimes and punishment to maintain order (obviously not currently), and we previously expunged perpetrators from society for crimes committed against others.

That set of plans and performances comes from our Creator. He created mankind; we broke the rules, He let us continue, but not without constraint. In our fallen nature, we have no limits. The rich and powerful have ruled through the ages, and still do. In our modern society, theft, lying, baby murders, and infidelity are examples that now go unpunished. So how do we respond in this kind of culture in which we live? It's OK if you DON'T DO IT TO ME!

This cultural environment, then, positions us to put up with what or whom we like and put off, whom we don't. I've done it for years. Have you? What's God's standard? Again, "FORGIVE AS THE LORD FORGAVE YOU." WOW, that's a challenge. Do I ever stop to ponder how much God has forgiven, and will continue, to forgive me? I have, but I need to perform it more aggressively. I'm banking on my Creator forgiving me into heaven. Are you?

One good way to show it is to pass on that forgiveness, TODAY!

FREEDOM 2021

Now that's a subject my culture has taken for granted. I was a history major in college on my way to Law School, and learned the concept of individual freedom. Did you know this was rooted in our Christian faith? All non-Christian cultures of the "ism's" lead to totalitarian, dictatorial governments such as the various empires, Germany in the past, and modern China as examples. No God (of the Bible), no freedom!

Christ was quoted as saying:" I am the way, the truth, and the life." (John 14:6). He earlier had stated that "the truth will set you free" (John 8:32). My suburban friends assume this to be true by experience, but take a trip to Cuba, Russia, or Iran today. Preach Christ on a street corner, and see if you make it back to the good ol' USA. In Christ's time on earth, it was the Roman empire and the Jewish religious system. People weren't free back then; anywhere!

Now you can get it. Christianity is the faith for freedom. People get "saved" when they repent and believe in the God of creation. The world system hates it when one expounds on their freedom from tyranny, earthly control systems, and the "wages" of sin. (Romans 6:23). It's the ultimate trip; looking forward to the ultimate trip; GET IT?

We are, however, asked to control ourselves in this life. In Galatians 5:13, the apostle Paul exhorts us, "do not use your freedom to indulge the sinful nature...Love your neighbor as yourself." So with what little time we have on his planet, serve forward. What do I mean by that you ask? Look out for the needs of others. Ezekiel 16:49 said Sodom was brought down because" they did not help the poor and needy."

One major drawing card to Jesus's following was the way He produced food. I'm sure there were farmer's markets back then, but they were seasonal. Jesus was able to catch fish at will, and feed 4000, and 5000 at His gatherings. Most would listen to anything He had to say. Ever been to a church potluck? In my youth in Michigan, those farmer's wives could really fill the food bag. I learned to go to the end of the line as none of the old church ladies was there to criticize my heaped-up plates. ☺

So what's the essence of our (Christian) faith? Individual freedom! That's what the Pilgrims came to this country for. That's what our founders established independence for. That's what the revolutionary armies fought and died for. That's what the World wars of the 1900s were fought for: to ensure that freedom wasn't stomped out by Godless leaders of tyranny.

So what's the Genesis of freedom? The Creator! His Son, and the Holy Spirit have filled believers ever since. Why do we care? Why do we stand for the Star Spangled Banner, and the Doxology? I'll tell you why, it's for freedom. It's getting harder and harder to pass that on to our youth. Much like the game where a message is started at a line of people, and 10 people later, you see what the person at the end speaks out.

Please re-read the top again. Jesus Christ is the source of freedom. Repent today, and receive your personal freedom. Serve others, love others, and enjoy your freedom. "The TRUTH" will set you free!

FREEDOM #2 2021

"He set me free." I heard this in fellowship last Sunday, just before my friend David shared some thoughts on the topic of SALVATION. You need to get saved; from what? If Marx the Communist was correct, we need to be saved from religion. If the lifeguard's correct, it may be the deep end of the pool. Nooooooo, we're speaking of something way beyond those negative happenings in life. We need to be saved from eternal death.

Titus 3:1-8 pretty much covers the topic. It does say to obey the government (and that's been a lot tougher lately), but Paul lived in Roman times. It moves on to being "disobedient, deceived, and enslaved, by passions"... And then speaks of "malice, envy, and being hated"... then" and love of God our Savior appeared, He saved us"... Do you see what He saved us from?

In the first 3 chapters of Genesis, we see we were created in freedom. Our representatives (Adam and Eve) were given total freedom and dominance if they only DIDN'T do one thing. But they did it. We've paid the price ever since. We must therefore be "saved" back to that freedom, and it lasts eternally. As stated, we're entrapped. But the vast majority doesn't see it, feel it, or buy into it. To the unsaved, Las Vegas is a trip to heaven, at least until the checkbook is balanced.

So this world system has been tampered with, and turned over to new management (in the garden). Some of us have been blessed with seeing that and are "under new (or old!) management"! There is no question in the mind of most incarcerated humans as to the difference between prison to freedom. When one "gets set free" (I am told), it can be a blessing! Some others are entrapped by an attitude that soon takes them back to prison.

But for the smart (Born Again) prisoners, it's a step into a new life, consciousness, and energy. Read John 3, and praise the Creator for the freedom offered, freedom paid for, and freedom everlasting. Understand that God our Creator extends forgiveness for all 10 Commandment failures, and then He forgets.

Get on the freedom train, and ride the rails through life and eternal existence. God laid the tracks, and He "sets" the schedule. Take Heavens express as you travel this earth, and you can also say: "free at last, free at last, thank God, I'm free at last." ☺

FRIENDSHIP AND FAMILY 2021

FRIEND (Webster): one attached to another by respect or affection. An acquaintance. One who is not hostile.

I was listening to my friend Chris present a study on the Biblical book of James recently. I call it the "do it" book of the Bible. If you believe it, do it. The greatest challenge I've had in my believing life, is living my faith out. Just ask my friends, family, competitors, business competitors, golf buddies, church acquaintances, enemies (?), etc. But I've known and experienced this for decades. I now look back in decades as I've had a couple bad ones but.... a number of really good ones.

Decades of great times with the kids and grandkids, and a number of great times with the wife. Many great experiences in my business ventures and career and great experiences traveling hither and yon. I've also seen everything from frustration, to sadness, to ugliness with those same individuals and ventures over time. So now I share, after eight decades, what seems to have carried me through: FRIENDSHIP

I looked ahead in the James study and saw a verse that leaped out to me. Reading Scripture is like digging for gold. When God opens a verse to you, it's like finding a nugget. You can pass over a verse time and again, but when the Holy Spirit has one for you, it's like being illuminated with neon lights. This one was verse 24in the 2nd chapter. .... "and he was called a friend of God" WOW, The Creator of the universe is so personal that He comes to a person named Abraham, of His creation, and considers him a friend?

God considers him a friend. I want some of that. I consider I got that with my salvation. I needed to be saved. Friendship helps that, and I guess we need it. Most of the creation seeks that from others, but it doesn't seem to work all that well. Can you fill your left hand with true friends, your Christian friends? Can you keep them for life? When God is your friend, His friendship is forever. I want some of that!

There's a great love exchange in the book of Solomon's Song. In Chap 5: 10-16, this lady describes her love as one handsome Adonis (aren't we all?) and ends her thoughts, "this is my beloved, and this is my friend" WOW, what a chic ☺. That's the kind of friendship/love every created human thinks about in life. That's why most people keep looking and looking and looking to a fault, or faults. It would be beautiful if one's spouse fulfilled that role, but it seldom works out that way.

So when you finally find a friend, keep them. Covet Christian friends who include Christ in the relationship. Develop the friendship. Nurture the relationship. Some say I was once close to my Creator, but not so much now. GUESS WHO MOVED? When you gain a friend, keep them. Good times (easy), bad times (not so easy). Invest! Life is short (I have eight decades of experience now). Make it/them count.

One last thought: Christ said in John 15:14, "you are my friends if you do what I command you." "Love (agape') one another." John 15 totally covers the subject.

And hope for, at the end, God says welcome (YOUR NAME), I consider YOU, my friend !!!

GETTING OLD! USE IT AND LOSE IT 2021

One of the joys of aging, is all the things you have learned in life so that one experiences the joys of experience. Sometimes it ain't so good, buy these can be masked with the better ones. Christ had great memories in life only to have them obliterated as a human, as He hung on the cross. With the ascension, in Acts 1, however, the experience of that day had been overcome by the resurrection, and His rocket ship removal.

Have you had bad times in life, potentially horrible? I can't say horrible, like my friends who went to Viet Nam, but I've lost businesses, my firstborn, homes, etc. During the same time, I've been saved, had kids saved and grandkids saved, traveled extensively in the free world, which I loved, and had a successful and sometimes happy marriage. The bad experiences hurt, but the good overcame them!

Have you ever seen old people jokes? I've laughed soooo hard I had to change my underwear sometimes. The truth is, I now can't remember half of what I did last week, but I can remember a lot of what I've studied over the past 50. How is that possible? I think Christ explained it to the disciples in John 16, right before He faced human condemnation: "I have said these things to you, that when the hour comes, YOU MAY REMEMBER THAT I TOLD THEM TO YOU"!

So I guess I get to USE it, "and" LOSE it. I happen to be a college graduate with a year of post-graduate work but no Masters. I've spent the 50 + years since then studying the Bible. It's written to assist me in Living, Learning (about God), and Loving (others). For me, it's worked at least half the time. It also taught me about something called my sinful nature. I.E., my personality, which wants to do what God, my Creator, doesn't. You know, the Ten Commandments etc.?

So I've created these "1 Page Briefs." I am capsulizing Biblical concepts, statements, and truths, to pass on to my grandkids. They aren't going to read a book I send, but maybe a "1 Page Brief" about one. They won't be building a library of reading, but maybe a collection of "1 Page Briefs." So I keep creating. I pass muster by sharing with my pastors, share-group friends, and just plain friends. So far, the reviews are favorable, so I must have learned and remembered something.

Getting old can be funny. Enjoy it when you reach it, at some point, with all the corrective surgery, pills, and available exercise programs. Unfortunately, your senility will outlive your memory, intelligence, and body. Ask a 9th decader; It begins when you walk down the hall into a room, and can't remember why you went there in the first place. Life's downhill from there. However, God can bring things to memory for sharing, encouragement, and blessing others. His small pack of fishermen, tax collectors, and Jewish scholars testified to that in the New Testament, as they quoted a bunch of farmers, sheepherders, and jailbirds, from the Old Testament.

So I hope you can read a few of my "1-Page Briefs', and be blessed.

I'm signing out as I commence my 9th decade of experiences. ☺ OUCH!

GOD FEARING VS GODLESS 2021

Essentially, we were founded on the principle of individual freedom, recognized as a gift from our Creator (Declaration of Independence). It's no great surprise to the average born-again Christian, as those actions align with the principles and activities of rebellion against our Creator. In my lifetime, I've seen our society reach a 50% rate of divorce, teach evolution to our kids as opposed to creation, murder 60 MM unborn babies, and also propagate the principle that weather is dependent on mankind as opposed to our Creator and sustainer.

This has so evolved in society that those who now lead, have been developed "BY" this society which, for the most part, could care less about the God of the Universe. It doesn't work! There are still some "good" people around, and even in important places, who follow God-given principles. But what was the majority of voters/leaders, is now the minority. Basically, it's those who believe in the veracity of the Holy Bible, as opposed to those who don't. You might say we began with the 10 Commands/Constitution and have ended up with the Washington DC government.

I truly, truly see this as the crux of our contest today. I really believe it's the Christ versus the anti-Christ. It's the wheat and the tares. Do not read this and take pride in your faith and trust, and position. Proverbs 16:18. Don't fall! That fall is like a drop off the Grand Canyon in Arizona or Royal Gorge in Colorado. Don't be swallowed up by the Earth as the sons of Korah were in Numbers 16, for their unbelief. Stand tall, with faith in the Word, in the face of rebellion toward our Creator. There is a right and wrong (10 commandments), you know. Pick the ultimate winner.

In short, see this as a Spiritual battle. It always has been since creation. Look ahead and look up! Read Romans 13 as you observe the day-to-day politic. God is taking us down the path, pasture, or highway of life. He really is in control as He was with Moses over Pharaoh. He can still save children and part the sea. While Christians exist, our country can succeed. When we are taken away (1 Thessalonians 4), the world and its system can fully operate without Holy Spirit interference.

GOD KNOWS EVERYTHING OMNISCIENT
2021

I was present for a teaching by my friend David this past Sunday. He was teaching on the Body of fellowship and mentioned the churches of Revelation, in passing. I created a brief on Overcoming earlier and also focused on ecclesia in the process. God wanted me to see one other dimension, and David brought it up.

The teaching is that God Almighty "KNOWS." Knows what, you ask? Everything! How many times to we read in scripture that God knew this or that thought that no human being could. How many times did God the Son know this fact or that; that another human held secret. In Revelation 2 and 3, we see more examples of God's attention to the details of His creation. That's why I don't believe in global warming, without God, or elections, without God, or life and assuredly death, without God.

As we review the 7 churches of Revelation then, we see Him state: I know your deeds, I know your tribulation and your poverty, I know where you dwell, I know your deeds, I know your deeds, I know your deeds, I know your deeds. It sounds to me as though God knows what's going on in our lives.

Have you ever done something as a kid saying, I hope my parents don't find out? As a high school or college student saying, I hope my principal doesn't find out. As an adult, you might have said, I hope my spouse or boss doesn't find out. I've come to the conclusion that these well-placed personalities are there for our constraint, just like the police, to demonstrate that God indeed has an eye on us. I think He lists the 7 churches just to exhibit how personal the process is.

We now live in the age of recordings, both audible and visual. One of my TV favorites is a show depicting the FBI. By using up-to-date technology, they can just about track anyone through recordings, records, or cell transmissions. It's both fascinating, and scary. My point/realization is that the Creator of the universe, and DNA, has utilized this from the beginning.

I know, I know, I know, I know, I know, I know, I know! Do you get the point? Whoever, whatever, wherever God is, He knows! At this point in existence, I relish this thought. I appreciate His protection and guidance. But given all of the above, I really appreciate His Love and forgiveness.

I hope you KNOW WHAT I MEAN! ☺

GOD THE CREATOR: A TRILOGY OF EVENTS 2021

What really sets God apart? From one created being to another, let me suggest the obvious. He created me, I didn't create Him. Believe it or not, a large block of humans believe they created God, in their own minds, if not through the process of evolution. This is called existentialism in philosophy. Don't be fooled that we are self-created ourselves. If we perform this thought process without faith in our Creator, the potential creations are myriad.

So what does Scripture say? Genesis 1:1, "In the Beginning, God created the Heavens and the Earth." So Biblically speaking, God was behind it all. We can't explain or comprehend eternity, but are promised that eventuality. God identified Himself as the "I AM" in Exodus 3:14. And Jesus did in John 8:58. In Colossians 1:16,17, Christ is listed as that Creator, AND SUSTAINER.

Secondly, Genesis said we rejected God's rule for this blessing of life and fell away. He then "CREATED" the process for returning to Him. John 3 Covers the subject as Christ says we need to be BORN-AGAIN. This 2nd creation ushers us into eternity where we were originally intended to be. Mark 1:15 denotes the process/attitude when it states we need to "repent and be baptized." This process is the 2nd Creation of our new Spirit. In fact, the Holy Spirit enters us and replaces our dead spirit, called our flesh. It's an exciting, amazing, and accelerating event. And stays with and builds us as we go through life. It eventually leads us to heaven and "eternal" life.

The last "CREATION," then, is the new heaven and earth. That's correct; the old ones are burned up/ dissolved (2 Peter3: 9-13). AMAZING. They are replaced by the "new" heaven and earth that you can read about in Revelation 21 and 22. For the believer whose Spirit has been recreated, if you will, this revelation and preachment are very exciting. Read about it, and cry with joy and jubilation.

So we have now seen the 3 key elements from our Creator God. If one has rejected God's love, it will be nonsense to them. If accepted through repentance, belief, and baptism, evolution is nonsense. The Biblical picture then, shows our Creator and His 3 Creations: the world and us, our Spirits, and the new heaven and earth. It's all there so one can study it, and hopefully, you will be blessed.

I hope you got created! ☺

GOD THE HOLY SPIRIT 2021

Christ introduced the disciples to the Holy Spirit in John16. He detailed His (the HS) role and function to them and made the point that He (Christ) had to leave and that He would then send His fellow member of the Godhead. Christ stated beginning in verse 8: "when He comes, He will convict the world of guilt, in regard to sin, and righteousness, and judgment: in regard to sin, because men do not believe in me; in regard to righteousness, because I'm going to the Father, where you can see me no longer; and in regard to judgment, because the prince of this world now stands condemned (convicted). What did He mean?

Firstly, sin is missing the mark. When one shoots an arrow or rifle at the target, they hope to hit the bulls eye. If you miss that center spot, it is a matter of sin; small or great. Christ was saying that if you pass through life, no matter how good you are, and you miss out on Him, you've sinned; missed the bulls eye. It doesn't matter how "good" you are. Jesus is perfect. The Biblical test for eternal life and salvation is the substitution of Christ's sacrifice for your sins (Or poor shooting ☺).

Secondly, being righteous! While Christ was with them, the disciples kept a pretty clean slate. When they didn't (Peter's denial), Christ was there to forgive and forget. The Holy Spirit then came to enter us, join us, and guide us. In other scripture, we see where God's Spirit can appeal to Christ in heaven for forgiveness, and that wouldn't be possible for Christ on earth at one locale. Today millions, if not billions, can appreciate the presence of God the Holy Spirit, in constant unison with our beings to teach and guide us.

Thirdly, "in regard to judgment"! This is so cool. Judgment is such a big issue to any breathing human being. Ever been pulled over by a cop? How do I get out of this, you think? Ever get pulled over by God? How do I get out of this one? The reality is that one dimension of salvation is the end of judgment, not progressive minor judgments, but final everlasting judgment. Christ's visit to this domain, then, was to seal Satan's ultimate judgment. That ended with the horrific Cross experience, and RESURRECTION DAY!

So Christ left so that the Holy Spirit could come. Christ left the earth for heaven, and the Holy Spirit left heaven for earth, to abide, guide, and lead those who asked for help through this existence. He had finished His work. God's adversary was condemned, and it was time for the next set of disciples to "go to work." US!

So repent my reader. You missed the bull's eye(10 Commandments Exodus 20). Ask God to forgive you. HE WILL! Then watch and participate with God's Spirit, IN YOU, and enjoy the results.

Shooting instructions can be found in John 3. ☺

GOD'S MARKETING PROGRAM 2021

1)The Bible

2)Baptism

3)Communion

It's very common in the USA when businesses are set up to establish a marketing program. It's nothing new and sets a manual in place to go to market and sell one's product to awaiting clientele. It's not at all uncommon for people to hear about your product offering and not have an interest, even if it's "the greatest thing since sliced bread." So then, programs are designed, created, and implemented to sell as many items as you can produce; and then some.

Maybe God's the originator of that discipline? At any rate, let's touch on the Christian program for salvation and sales.

Firstly God gave us the Bible.

2 Tim 3:16 states that men were inspired by the Creator to speak for Him. That's His program, and the opportunity to accept His program for life success is written in significant detail. I've spent 50 years minimally, studying the subject, reading books, and attending school to learn His Word, and I feel I've at least cracked the surface. So learning, reading, and sharing what one has learned is the 1st phase of the program.

Secondly is Baptism:

If one hears the Word and hasn't been baptized, the 1st phase of the program probably hasn't taken place. In Acts 2:38, the apostle Peter preaches that we are to "repent and be baptized." In the 1st chapter of John, Jesus had John baptize Him. WHY? Very simply, that's the way we demonstrate the change in our lives. We have been cleansed from the curse of our sins (breaking God's rules), and been washed from head to toe(by the Holy Spirit). Have you been changed from the inside out? Let the world around you know.

Thirdly is Communion

In Matthew chapter 26, Jesus initiated the sacrament. He gave us a reminder of the unbelievable sacrifice He was about to experience. His body would be broken, and His blood would be spilled. It was so serious that Paul wrote in I Corinthians 11 not to take it lightly, as if one would. Well, they were in Corinth at the time, gorging at church potlucks and getting drunk. We are encouraged/commanded to take it only to appreciate the cost of our salvation and demonstrate to others what was accomplished by Christ for us.

So there you have it. This is God's marketing program. It's activated to share the program of salvation with others. We were created, we sinned, we were saved, and it's a great program we really want to share with everybody.

Everyone will die and face eternity. The Bible states that it will be eternal bliss, or eternal punishment. That's what it says! That sin life has to be punished by our Creator. Accept Christ's substitutional sacrifice for your sins (10 commandments), or receive your personal recompense.

It's a simple program that has now been marketed to you. Can I take your order???

GOD'S GLORY 2021

I went to my porch this past weekend and faced directly into a bright and shining full moon. I was surprised to have that same moon appear in the sky the following morning. What beauty, what majesty, what a glorious depiction of God's handiwork. In my human parlance of tactility, I imagined it hanging there, being placed there, being up there, or over there. In reality, in God's creation, in God's Word, it's just THERE.

It should be enough to quote Genesis 1:1 "In the beginning, God created the heavens and the earth." That speaks of an awesome and amazing power to create human beings. Our entire educational system has given up this revelation to follow the human creation of evolution. When one doesn't believe in God, they create alternative realities ad infinitum. What's truly amazing to any believer is that 80% of created humans could ignore the "revealed" for the "absurd."

As King David passed the baton to his son Solomon, and the privilege of erecting God's temple in Jerusalem, he evoked a prayer representing his faith. It's presented to us in 1 Chronicles 29:11: "Yours, oh Lord, is the greatness and the power, and the glory and the majesty and the splendor, for everything in heaven and earth, is yours. Yours, oh Lord, is the kingdom; you are exalted as head over all." Is that your prayer? Please re-read that prayer a few times.

When I saw that moon, and reflected on the awesomeness of it's just BEING THERE, I was mildly overwhelmed. It's just THERE. The earth is just HERE. The sun is just THERE. How much do I simply take for granted? The universe is soooo vast, and yet, it IS. We are reminded, educated, described to, and encouraged to extol, God's creation in the 1st chapter of Romans (one of my favorite chapters). In verse 20, we are told by Paul that what has been made by God is "enough" to verify God's existence. God's Glory then is manifested and exhibited in His creation. WOW!

And so, as I viewed the moon that clear October evening, I was awestruck. GOD'S GLORY. It was just THERE! It wasn't hanging there, placed there, over there, or up there. Yes, my friend, it was just THERE. God has created it and sustains it. Do you get it?

Re-read David's prayer until you do! ☺

REST: GOD STARTED IT. KEEP IT UP 2021

"In the beginning, God created." And after He finished, He rested (Genesis 2:2, 3). God amped that up in the 10 Commandments when He attached it to a Sabbath day of rest! He then referred to His Creation (Exodus 20:8). In other words, God created everything, and when finished, He created "REST." Rest isn't something that exists by happenstance. It's a real period of space that the Creator gave us as a regular activity. Read the "turns" in Ecclesiastes 3.

I have garnered 3 basic appeals to resting given by God. They have a created purpose. There is also the factoid that God leads by example. The three are then: 1) The rest from creation, 2) The rest from the toils of life, and 3) The rest from this life into eternity where God lives. In our first 2 decades, we need rest from youthful exuberance, studies, and maybe the newness of labor and production toward provision. In the next 4 decades, we dream of rest from life's toils and the daily grind.

I dreamt of this in my 6th decade, working at headquarters. I thought, "if only they had a resting room where I could take a power nap each day, I could work until 7 pm with energy to boot." Christ said, "I will give you rest" (Matthew 11:28-30). He spoke of a yoke that He would share, while you labored pulling the plow. The equipment has changed, but the concepts are still in place.

The 3rd arena of REST, then is our promised eternal life. Isaiah is a great read describing this. In the New Testament, one can focus on Revelation 21 and 22. Another poignant verse (Hebrews 4: 8-11) exhorts us to believe, to both encourage and warn us. Even the Apostle Paul couldn't wait:" For to me, to live is Christ, AND TO DIE IS GAIN" (Philippians 1:21).

So I guess rest is of significance to a Biblical Christian. Regard God for our/His creation. Take note of His rest. Take a break or design a break into your life-long process/career. Look forward and plan for your eternal reward and the rest it affords. Share that information with neighbors and friends, and of course, FAMILY. For the most part, you will get rejection. Over 80% of all people end up rejecting information concerning the Creator God of the Bible and His reality.

It's a hostile world we're created into. We make up gods, we long for material gain, we murder our unborn creations, we battle each other, we take credit for the weather, and we credit ourselves today with advances in technology, health, and longevity.

It's time for a God rest, dear reader. Realize from whence we came, and where we're going. Use your intelligence, but add a dose of God's Word, a pound of Godly Fellowship, and a ton of Loving Ministry. When you rest, you will love it, and when this life is over, you will get that ETERNAL REST God promised!

IN THE MEANTIME, PLAN AN OCCASIONAL REST! IF IT WAS GOOD ENOUGH FOR GOD...

GOING GLOBAL 2021

This "brief" covers a most relevant aspect of end times (eschatology) today. Between 2000 and 4000 years ago, God's written WORD spoke of a time in our world system when globalization would be created as a system of unity for all mankind who were Godless. Essentially, all nations would come together under a specific leader for the good of mankind. It happened to the Babylonians, Persians, Egyptians, and Roman Kingdoms, in their day. The difference was the size of the world "systems" in those days. The next big one, then, will cover the entire globe,

God projected this economic and political system, and if you will, religious system, in the book of Revelation. Its leader is called "the Antichrist" by the Apostle John. We now live in the times unknown at the writing of Scripture, when the global world and its system are working toward unification. The United Nations, climate change, G7, and air flights have experienced where one can fly from the USA to Europe in 1 hour.

In Daniel 9:27, "he" (the world leader) makes a covenant "with the many" for world peace. In 2 Thessalonians 2:3, he is named again. In Matthew 24:14 and15, Christ predicts the whole world's revelation of the Gospel, and this world leader, taking a seat in the temple of Jerusalem as a self-proclaimed god. This, then, becomes a global experience in defiance of the Creator God of the universe.

We now see a world prophesied that, for the time being, has no Christians (the Rapture). Studies conjecture as to what follows this event. The great tribulation and God's judgments for an unbelieving world do certainly take place. One hundred years ago, no one in Kansas would have given a moment's notice to Israel or Afghanistan. Today, they milk the headlines. Space ship trips by the world's billionaires are front page. Anything global is everyone's concern.

The world has gone global. Israel exists. (Ezekiel 39: 25-29). The 3rd Jewish temple is on the architect's drawing board. The Earth is shaking, and the waters are shifting. Food is a major concern as the world has vast supplies and can't get it distributed, leading to the daily deaths of 25,000 people (Google it). As regional crises continue, they are no longer considered "just" regional.

And so, my reader, be ready. A Christian, born-again, believer needn't fear! The Lord is preparing His return. Based on a global mentality today, we are prepared for the prophecy mandates, as listed in Scripture. The Bible insists that Christ will return. Are you enlightened and excited? Are you prepared? Have you shared this with your friends and neighbors?

Everybody's global in 2021.

GOOD THEOLOGY VS. BAD THEOLOGY

2021

We have been studying other religions and faiths the past few weeks, and it struck me that Biblically speaking, people in general, and in particular, enjoy faiths and religions of their own choosing. What we come to realize when judging by our perspective of God's Word is that we share some interpretations and applications, and disagree on many others.

It seems to me that the key chapters for perspective and separation are John 3 in the gospels for salvation, and 1st Corinthians 15 in the Epistles for the Gospel. We learn that to be with Christ for eternity, we must be "born again" in the Spirit and that the good news from that is that Christ proved there is life after death by His unwarranted death and resurrection in propitiation for our faults.

I, therefore, conclude that my Catholic, Baptist, Presbyterian, Methodist, and other Christian-based faiths agree in the area of good, basic, Gospel theology. (Nicene Creed) Those who belong to those particular religions, and understand the aforementioned chapters, share in the arena of good theology. To not share in those basic beliefs would deny the blood sacrifice mentioned and would be a denial of the essence of the faith, and therefore denote bad theology.

Let me add further, that each of the above has added to the basic gospels one way or another; the Catholics foremost. Others add that one shouldn't dance, drink alcohol, sprinkle baptize, and worship Mary as Christ's equal. The scale goes from the innocent to the abhorrent. What bad theology does is that it cuts short the true gospel of grace, and begins shifting the weight of salvation away from Christ and over to us. Whether minor or major in action or thought, this becomes a significant move from the true gospel, and, therefore becomes a salvation dependent on our actions and not our faith in Christ's.

The final and "other" group then deals with totally bad theology. They are any and all religions which deny the Deity of Christ and the Gospel. It's amazing to me that 80% of mankind is in this position. Only 20% of living beings are a part of the Christian religion, and who knows how many are born again. That means we have a great deal of work ahead, and are told that the fields are ripe for harvest.

We must therefore drive earnestly to learn the Word (the Bible), share the Word, and defend the Word (John 1). We must come together based on good theology, and serve God in the process. We must seek to defend against bad theology, which inhibits the truth and limits Christ's Holy Spirit from effective ministry. We've been blessed by Grace (Ephesians 2: 8, 9), with Grace, through Grace, and too many born-again Christians don't appreciate the significance of their position.

We need to strive for that appreciation in thought and action!

GPS: Finding Directions in Life   2021

The other day, my wife suggested I check my car radio for street directions to a restaurant we wished to visit. Now I've owned this vehicle for the past 5 years and never bothered to use my GPS. We live in the Phoenix area, and compared to NYC, Chicago, and LA, where we've lived over the years, it's been a pleasure for me to get around with so little traffic or confusion.

Nonetheless, I gave it a shot and booted it up. This nice lady began the instructions out loud and guided us to the location directly. It gave me pause to think this service has been available to me from the beginning of ownership, and I never utilized it. All I had to do was open the service, follow the guidelines, and be guided to wherever I wished to go. She even instructed me where to turn and when I'd be getting to the intersection.

I decided to compare this to the Bible. GPS: "God's Perfect Solution" for getting through life, where to turn, and getting me to my final destination. It made me think of how many people have an old family Bible in the house they never utilize either. I asked for a Bible at a friend's the other day, because I wanted to share a verse with them. The cover was covered in dust, so I blew it off, and the dust spoofed up in the air. It was available but unused, just like the GPS in my car.

In 2 Timothy 3, the scripture is referred to as "living and active." For those who have studied it, there is no question concerning that truth. It states from where we came, how to get around where we are, and eventually, where we are going. It's profound and affects the ignorant and the educated. Unlike great books, highly pedigreed philosophies, and learned institutions and their graduates, it remains available to the less educated, from whence it originated. God does have a sense of humor, because we do, and with a few exceptions, He picked the least educated to share His thoughts with the entirety of human Creation.

So if, by chance, you've been meandering through existence (life) and would like a little bit (or a lot) of direction, just GPS your Creator. The ride may be quicker, smoother, more directionally correct, but lastly, more satisfying, and, if discerned correctly, you will end up in the right place. (This infers there is a wrong place, you know).

GPS hasn't always been available. It's a very recent phenomenon. The Bible has only been available to the common man for the last 500 years, even though written 2000-5000 years ago. What's your excuse? Like me, are you just ignoring this satellite's available service and guidance track, or are you just refusing the available service? If, eventually, you end up in the wrong location, after years of traveling by the seat of your pants, it will be sad!

Then may I encourage you. Activate this "living and active" service today. GPS your future before you arrive, potentially, where you don't wish to be.

Bring God's GPS into your life.

HANDLING SUCCESS! (THE CHURCH SCENE) 2021

Are you part of a growing church? Are more people coming? Is it tougher finding a parking space? Need more room for the kiddies? I hope so. What kind of a church do you have? They are all listed in the 2nd and 3rd chapters of Revelation. They only have one thing in common, most members "overcome/conquer." The other people who attend, join, check in, and feel religious satisfaction by attending, are just players. In our culture today, it's not necessary to attend for social pressure anymore. In fact, there's more pressure to not attend, and go to the church of the "little league."

The key, then, is the focus of the church. You might call it the basic mandate for the church's being, and I would wrap it in the pyramid package along with the Trinity triangle of Father, Son, and Holy Spirit. The church triangle then is Theology, Fellowship, and Ministry. Theology...............

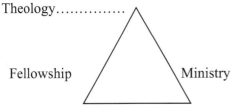

One might best express it as Theology: what is "taught," Fellowship: what is "sought," and Ministry, what is "wrought."

"Theology" is the critical element for all "born again" fellowships. Most churches are taught with preachments. I would call the preferred exhortation to be exegetical verse by verse, by chapter, by Book teaching. This focus attempts to be inclusive of God's thoughts; the writer's intended exhortation, and cross-reference theology with other scripture references. From time to time, topical series meet the specific needs of a fellowship that leaders/teachers/elders hopefully focus toward. Good Theology will always be a draw for church growth.

"Fellowship" is the satisfaction that "born again" believers crave. I think, and have experienced, that catching people when they come is the key. If possible, gatherings (like the old Sunday Schools) are a great fellowship time. The old church potluck is great. Men's and women's fellowships around tables are super. Share groups or growth groups away from the church are a mandate for fellowship in a growing church. The key to successful growth is people meeting people, people sharing with people, people praying with people, and Christians socializing with fellow Christians.

Thirdly, I believe that no successful ministry is worthwhile without missions/ministry, as the third point of this Trinity. "Ministries" are wrought as metal is with a blacksmith. It's the banging, clanging, shaping, molding, and giving part of any successful group of believers. Help another church plant, take some kids to camp, dig a well in an area where people walk miles for putrefied water when 1000's of fresh drinkable gallons of water are right below their feet. Teach people how to grow crops, and raise poultry and animals for ongoing consumption. Ministry is "wrought," and is the only goalpost of successful church growth and value.

So are you a part of a successful church? Does it lay out the culture for these three in a country where attention has been shifted to Godless government to achieve what our Creator and Savior has ordained?

What is TAUGHT will lead to what is SOUGHT, by the ones who develop what is WROUGHT. God has a purpose for every fellowship created in Jesus' name.

HELP IT GROW!

HOPE 2021

This word represents an expectation and desire for a particular thing to happen. It basically drives us each day as grown-up humans to face the day awake and the life not yet seen. The great Christian theologian of the 1900s, Francis Schaeffer explained it: Christianity is realistic because it says that if there is no TRUTH, there is also no HOPE. So then, reading about the TRUTH (the Bible) and learning who the TRUTH is (Jesus) John 14:6 will grow our hope for life.

All through my life, I have hoped. I hope I make the team; I hope I graduate; I hope she says yes, and I hope I get that job. Hope gives us purpose or at least drives our purpose. If you lose it, the project is over, or in the extreme, even your life. Suicide is the worst of human dilemmas, and it's the result of hope ending. There's a famous reminder in verse: One can live 40 days without food, 10 days without water, 60 seconds without air, BUT NOT 1 SECOND WITHOUT HOPE.

God's WORD is rich in HOPE! "Rejoice in hope" (Romans 12:12, "the hope of Glory" (Colossians 1:27), "waiting for our blessed hope (Titus 2:13), and "to be born-again to a living hope(1Peter1:13), which brings me to my view after a robust almost 9 decades of this life. As Paul inked to the Colossians: "the HOPE laid up for you in Heaven" (Colossians 1:5) GET IT???

One of the main drives for Christians in this, or any age, has always been the hope factor. Have you ever heard a non-believer speak of any desire at all to see this existence end in favor of entering into an eternal destiny of freedom, favor, and happiness? It's hard to get many Believers to focus on this eventuality as written about in Revelation 21, 22. And yet, any materially blessed human will go on and on about a planned vacation to beaches, cruises, or party towns. We all share that thinking about this world; why not the next world?

So hope is a very big thing to our psyche! If you have lived in the past century, it's what drives American humans to continue. It's what drives immigrants to our shores for a better (this) life. But most of all, it's what drives born-again Christians to think about, pray about, and act as if this earthly life just isn't all that there is.

How far forward is your thinking? Do you have your sights on heaven? The writer Paul in the New Testament did. He stated:" To live is Christ, to die is GAIN" (Philippians 1:21). If the author of 13 New Testament chapters felt that way, and came to that conclusion as led by the Holy Spirit, then I'm all in. If he's wrong, I'll suffer the consequences, but I'll lay my wager on the Bible and the Holy Spirit.

Where is your hope? Human beings are said to have 3 basic hopes, if not in God's thoughts: Power, Praise, and Possessions. Think about it, and you'll agree. In our country, citizens work for a better position, some adulation from others, and the assurance of enough wealth to retire comfortably with checks or social security plus.

But as born-again Christians, we look ahead again. We don't look at what's left behind (toys and stocks and real estate) but what we take with us (BODY, SOUL, AND SPIRIT).

Give it some thought, dear reader, and get "ALL ABOARD" on the "HOPE" train. ☺

HOW DOES ONE GET TO HEAVEN? One must be BORN AGAIN

I have a few friends who love to camp out. As a grade-schooler, I was raised in Michigan. It was very common for friends to hunt, fish, and camp out. For those friends, it was very important to build a campfire for warmth, light, and cooking. For the last 20 years, I've lived in California and Arizona. The last thing one wants to do here is to build a fire. So, where am I going with this?

To build a great fire, it's good to have paper as a starter. A good start for this would be the normal family Bible. It's essentially a used-less book lying around with little or no use. Incredibly it's a book of information on where life comes from, is, and where it's going. Due to a pandemic scare of recent, people have been excessively anxious about where they are (as well as how far apart) and a little about where they are going. They still watch TV, read novels, and go to the movies. Because they are afraid to die, they are getting vaccines, wearing masks, standing 6 ft apart, and getting upset with people who don't.

I live with a couple thousand people in a gated community enclave of 55+ individuals. I shoot pool with a handful of seniors whose average age is 80+. We made it through at this point, but it's safe to say we'll all be gone in a decade. Where I'm going is crucial to me; because I know. My acquaintances don't seem to care. If they read the aforementioned Bible, they would. We escaped the pandemic, but we won't escape the end of old age. It's a fact of existence.

So what about the great fire starter that I mentioned? *Learn it or burn* it. It's better than a good novel. Before bed, it's a fantastic read and helps me sleep better. (great at my age). Plenty of very good movies have been made with the Bible as a reference. But it's a take it or leave it scenario. If you take it, the promises are fantastic. If you leave it, have a good time camping.

My sister and I shared about old age once. I asked her where she thought she was going after this life. She hoped for heaven. I told her I had a guarantee. In the book called John, chapter 3, verse 16, it is written, "For God so loved the world, that He gave His only Son, that whoever believes in Him should not perish, but have eternal life." I grabbed onto that belief years ago. It didn't make me a better person, but I at least figured out what kind of guy I was and that I needed to be forgiven by my Creator, for just a few things, PAST, PRESENT, and FUTURE.

Earlier in verse 3, Jesus had said to a religious leader, "unless one is BORN AGAIN, they cannot see the Kingdom of Heaven." You can pull that book off the shelf and dust it off. It's got a lot more to say about life (past, present, and future). If you're reading this "brief," there is still time. It's a choice, I guess. If you do choose to go camping, take this book for fire paper. As you rip out the pages for kindling, read a couple verses. You might be surprised at what God wants to share with you.

SEE YOU IN HEAVEN??? I'm told that the alternative is not a camping trip!!!

ICONS OR NOTHING 2021

Most people appreciate good architecture, art, or expression. I ask personally, what's happened to Christian architecture? For perspective, I've lived in Chicago, New York, and been to Europe. Moody church is a great old giant worship center in Chicago. St Patrick's in NYC is a beautiful cathedral. Westminster Cathedral in London, Notre Dame in Paris, cathedrals in Portugal, and of course, the Basilica in Rome with its statuary and the ceiling of the Sistine Chapel by Michelangelo.

I personally believe that the Catholics go too far with their icons and the non-Biblical worship of Mary. But the grandeur of the Cathedrals is an amazing visitation. Some were built in 100's of years, with incredible arches to observe. The stained glass windows portraying Christ have blessed multitudes throughout the centuries, and still do today.

I can't imagine how a visit to the Temple in Jerusalem could have felt, or a stopover at Solomon's house would have awed. In a church service in So Denver each week, I was able to view the Rockies. I was blessed by the splendor of God's creation mentioned in Romans 1, as I worshiped each week. I visit a church in Gold Canyon off and on to enjoy the view of the Superstitions, organ music, bell ringers, and a choir of 40-50 joyful, old noise makers, and the time of worship is a blessing.

Sadly, to me, it seems that Arizona churches have given in to blackness and nothingness. Blackness may be due to the expense of A/C out here. The offset today is a heavy dose of Audio/Visual work with Icons superimposed to the screens. What is missing for me is the main reminder of Christ's suffering for me, and the structure from where He eventually was resurrected; the Cross.

In our fellowship, for years, we had an old rugged cross off the front ceiling draped with a red scarf. It was a great focus, especially during communion and baptism. These two commemorations are the main outside drawing cards in God's marketing program and were the last two agendas Christ gave His disciples to "do in remembrance of Me." Important? I think so.

So please do it sparingly. But do it! Then we can remember when gathered together, or just stopping by for a prayer, just what it was that was done for us.

J.O.Y. JOY TO THE WORLD 2021

I learned about acronyms a little late. I took post-graduate courses at UCLA and Seminary. One course was in church history, and I got a tip to draw a picture first, name it, and use the letters for key memory sentences. An example was a rock: picture it, use R.O.C.K., and write sentences. My first history test was an essay test. I was done in 45 minutes and walked out. Later, I heard the next classmate left in 1 ½ hrs. My grade was A+.

So let's go to work on the exercise of life. The acronym I'm going to use is JOY. The letters represent:

Place Jesus First, others Second, and Yourself third! If we all followed this little word and its true meaning, we wouldn't need counselors. Most people live life spelling the word YOJ (if the J is even used). In the morning, the first question asked might be, "what am I going to do today"? Not what am I going to do for others today or what am I going to do for my Creator? Get it?

How about Jesus first? In Matthew 6:33, we are exhorted to: "But seek first His Kingdom, and His righteousness, and all these things shall be added to you." All what things? How about Life, Liberty, and the pursuit of happiness? How about prosperity? (Ecclesiastes 7:14). In parts of this world, owning a chicken makes one prosperous. In my neighborhood, owning a house and a car makes one prosperous, and then some.

How about Others second? John 13:35 admonishes us to "…have LOVE for one another." When one is focused outward instead of self-ward, they have very little time for pity parties. And once those parties begin, they are difficult from which one can entangle. The average person needs be counseled out of them, which one might call the Dr. Phil syndrome. Pastor Tim at our fellowship has a full docket of you-first'ers each and every week. It's good that he is there. It would be better if he could work his way out of the vocation.

How about YOURSELF third? That's where I am today. I don't have everything I want out of this life, not by a long shot. I'll skip the details. However, when I put Jesus 1st, and others 2nd, myself as 3rd, it seems to work out. Every once in a while, I slip and put myself 1^{st,} satisfying my nature to sin. However, it generally proves to be impractical, even in the short run. I've found that when exercising #3 first, it's good to return to #1.

I think Solomon covered it well in Ecclesiastes. See God as your provider. The challenge for him in this life was just that. When one goes off on their own without God in mind as one's Creator and provider, #2 may happen, and #3 tends to rise to the lead slot. So get your counting in sequence. As management guru Peter Drucker taught, do first things first.

Set your acronym today. Live a life of JOY: JESUS FIRST, OTHERS SECOND, and YOURSELF THIRD.

Try it; you'll like it! ☺

JOY OF THE LORD #2 2021

Have you ever considered incarceration or torture? I have, from time to time, and did recently, as I heard of the people who attacked the nation's capitol as they were caught up in the enthusiasm at a D.C. rally. They broke some windows, entered offices, and flat-out scared the Congress people to death (one way to get rid of some of them) as they met in chambers. Were they correct in their overzealous enthusiasm? I think not. A peaceful march in the spirit of MLK would have sufficed, I think. Nonetheless, a lady was killed, some guards died of stress, and the congress ran for the hills in fear.

Of course, some of the assailants were placed in jail, but their forgotten souls are still imprisoned. And some are lightly tortured for rejecting vaccines and are kept from presenting bail. Meanwhile, buildings in the West were burned, people were killed, and cities were surrendered by mobs. Nobody's in jail! I thought to myself, could I handle being in a 10 x 10 cell for 10 months? For a demonstration?

This morning I viewed a Christian show where they discussed people around the world that were sent to jail, and solitary confinement, just for their expression of their Christian faith. Stories have surfaced that many have the common response of " the Joy of the Lord." The JOY of the Lord? Do they mean like Paul and Silas or the Apostle Peter? I think/guess so! How else could one lose their freedom as many have over the years in foreign lands? But this is the United States.

When the returned Jews in Israel grumbled, Nehemiah exhorted them in chapter 8:10: "Do not grieve, for the Joy of the Lord is your strength." Do you need that encouragement today? Are your circumstances insurmountable? Time flies, just like circumstances, like a bad boss, like an illness, and I submit, like depression: IF (?), you allow JOY to master your life.

In John 16:20, Christ tells the disciples: "your grief will turn to JOY." In Hebrews 12:2, we read of Christ's example: "who for the Joy set before Him, endured the cross, scorning the shame, and sat down at the right hand of the throne of God."

So don't downplay the power of Joy and anticipation. Study God's Word, and appreciate His presence, power, and peace. Bring His world of open freedom into your prison of life, and you will escape your dungeon, as did the disciples. Ask Jesus into your life as a manager, and not just a visitor.

BRANCH OUT INTO ETERNITY! ☺

James 3 (Teaching the Bible)

To teach: to cause to know something …   to impart the knowledge of…

To me, James seems to "DIVIDE" his book in chapter 3 with an admonition against weaker Christians' teaching. Teaching Scripture seems to be a qualified responsibility that God wants to guide. In chapter one, he says if you lack wisdom, "ask God." He castigates "double-mindedness." He speaks of "helping the helpless," and not being stained by the world. He points out the purity of God's Law by stating the breakage of one law is the guilt of all. He uses the extreme example of Abraham's potential sacrifice of his son Isaac as the Supreme act of "friendship" with God.

Without a tongue, one can't teach. He focuses on chapter 3 then, pointing out the power of the tongue as a purveyor of good or evil! He gets into attitude, if you will. He contrasts worldliness with heavenliness, if you will. Is it my way, or God's way? Is it worldly wisdom, or wisdom from above? The main value of church fellowship and teaching, then, is to learn more about Godly wisdom and not worldly success. The tongue is compared to a ship rudder or a horse's bit in his mouth. Enough said.

One who aspires to teach should scrutinize this admonition. I have taught off and on over the years. Some of the off times were self-imposed periods when I enjoyed the world just a little too much. Other times, I wanted to teach, but didn't get the opportunity. Do you want to teach? Why? Does this admonition in James 3 trouble you? Good teachers are hard to find. Qualified teachers are even harder to find. But there are people out there, just as the disciples whom God had prepared.

The whole point of James' book, I believe, is if you believe it, live it. If you're going to teach it, live it. However, if you're struggling with the application of your faith, for your friend's sake, don't teach it. And to ice this Spiritual cake, if you choose to teach, expect a stricter judgment. The joy of our ultimate faith is steadfastness mentioned in chapter 1, perfect and complete.

Sharing, then, becomes a blessing for you and others, at home, in the neighborhood, at your table at men's fellowship, etc. Nothing is worse than sharing by people inadequate to the task. The disciples were not learned men. But they did spend 3 years with our Lord, and were empowered by the Holy

LIVING A GREAT LIFE   2021

This weekend would have been perfect if only the Phoenix Suns had won their playoff game in the NBA. Oh well!

To capsulate, I heard 3 messages on our interaction with other humans and how we should approach those, live with others, and practice the highest ideals. I heard 3 presentations, which one might see as the trinity of good fellowship. I have studied this over the past 5 decades, and the proof is in the ongoing

Truth of scripture.

Firstly, my pastor, Costi, cited I Peter 3. After hearing, that wives are well guided to have a submissive attitude and life, in action, and men need to sacrifice for their spouse as Christ did for the church, I realize there is no favoritism. The chapter goes on to activity with fellow Christians, and Costi listed 6 "be's." Be of one mind, be sympathetic, be biased toward church fellowship, be compassionate, be humble, and be without vengeance. The list is in chapter 3:8,9. Why? So you can "inherit a blessing."

The next morning Pastor Chuck spoke from Colossians 3. He pictured the Christian life like a teeter-totter. He pictured us on one end, and the Holy Spirit on the other seat. How nice when He is up for us, and how awful when we are in charge. Chapter 3 covers it quite well. Verse 11, then sums up the Christian's response to the WOKE culture in which we live. It's not one human vs. another, but Christ, "who is all, and in all." We don't have a racial divide, but rather a Spiritual divide.

Finally, my pastor friend David spoke out of the Book of Jude to "those who are loved by God and kept by Jesus Christ." The little book/chapter ends with a great doxology: "To Him who is able to keep you from falling, and to present you before His glorious presence without fault and with great JOY---to the only God our Savior be glory, majesty, power, and authority, through Jesus Christ our Lord, before "ALL ages," now and forevermore, AMEN!

So it's not where one starts up, but rather where one ends up. We look to our Creator to "save" us, "protect" us, and "keep" us. To us, life is a lengthy process. It seems like we trudge forward in hip waders through deep thick sludge. The strange thing for me, at least, is that looking back, I picture myself at the base of a ski slope when I visualize the life I've experienced. With that experience, I'm led to exhort my children, grandchildren, youthful friends, and acquaintances, to work and follow the admonitions given in the above chapters. I will guarantee that even though the process may still be drudgery, the look back will be utterly Joyful.

If you are blessed, at this stage, to have our Creator in your life, let Him lead you through the "process." You won't always be happy, but you will always be/feel blessed. There are lists of right things to do, and lists of wrong things to not do. You will always be a work in process. Hang in there! I thank God repeatedly, that I have a Bible. I have my 20 yr old Bible with prolific underlining. I'm amazed how many times that Sunday messages are already underlined, and yet they always seem new and fresh.

Enjoy the journey/process. I pray that the end makes your process worthwhile.

LIVING WITH (IN) SIN 2021

One of the saddest commentaries that we learn in life is the first few chapters of the Proverbs. What's actually a learned advantage for any Christian is the constant battle with what is called, by the Bible, SIN! It is broadly defined in …. As "whatever is not of FAITH" (Romans 14:23). Faith in what? Or to what? To the Born-again Christian, that personage and set of principles are the Creator and His stated rules and guidelines for living through this life.

I recently surveyed the first few chapters of King Solomon's Proverbs. In chapter 6, He listed the oft-noted 7 deadly sins. Have you read them lately? All Christians, at some time, have reviewed the Ten Commandments (Exodus 20)and thanked God for forgiveness. Christ pointed out that even "thinking about" breaking the big 10 is a sin (Matthew 5:28). WOW, that's a tough mandate given by our Creator and God. I can't think of a day in the recent past that I haven't considered a lie, a minor theft, of some lust, or in my younger days, hating someone, dishonoring my parents, or swearing God's name. Thank God for forgiveness.

So what does God list in Proverbs 6, which He hates? Try on "haughty eyes" (lust), a lying tongue, "murder," "a heart that devises wicked plans," "feet that run to evil," "a false witness who breathes out lies," and one who sows discord among brothers." Well, I guess one has a good chance to make it through each day, if you just get a Godly book, hide in your reading room, and pray. But most of us get up, go out, and mix with others every day, and that's where our faith meets application.

In chapter 3, a well-known verse is oft-quoted: "Trust in the Lord with all your heart, and lean not on your own understanding. In all your ways acknowledge Him, and He will direct your paths." My friend Terry had our SS class memorize that 50 years ago, and I never forgot it. Thank you Terry! Later on, in chapter 8:13, we read, "the fear of the Lord, is hatred of evil." God spends a good deal of script focusing on adultery up to that point. I believe it's due to the thought of "cheating" on God. You know, where you say you have faith and then get greedy for money, or are tempted by your lust toward a friend's wife, or wished you had a better house and car, like your neighbor or a larger retirement check like your friend.

All of these are covered in the above. Lastly, one might consider a common U.S.A issue; gluttony. Chapter 23:21 states: for the drunkard and the glutton will come to poverty." Consider San Francisco and Los Angeles today. In the midst of wealth and self-aggrandizement, we have the greatest homeless population per capita this side of India; can we say it any clearer today? As our society and culture turn their backs on God, are the results any different than Noah's day or Sodom and Gomorra?

We are encouraged/commanded to "seek this day who you will serve." That's our challenge, friend ☺. We are called the "bride of Christ." Rest in Him, and arrest your nature. Enjoy God's blessings in this life, but stay away from the forbidden fruit. AMEN? OR AMEN!

MARRIAGE AND FIDELITY: ACCORDING TO SCRIPTURE   2021

I was listening to a daily word from a pastor the other day and appreciated his good Spirit. I agreed with his points on marriage and sex in the 2020s, realizing our culture today in American society has loosened significantly of late. Shacking up is totally accepted. Gay marriage is prolific, accepted, and even performed in churches. Men and women can be labeled as they choose in spite of their birth genders. The ultimate extension, of course, is gay parenthood by insemination or adoption and inter-athletic competition.

When I was young, these activities would have been considered absurd in society, and a cause for mental analysis or incarceration. NO MORE! Infidelity is nothing new. Old Testament Patriarchs had affairs, multiple marriages, and divorce. So what scriptures can give us guidance? If I listen to our church elders, I will get good advice; for sure, but I think more scripture helps.

Let's begin at the beginning. In the Bible's 2nd Chapter, God says: "Therefore, a man shall leave his father and his mother and hold fast to his wife, and they shall become one flesh." I was surprised by the use of "wife." God said to "leave your father and mother and take your wife." Very obviously, God meant that we have a very "significant other" in our lives. No agreements were mentioned, and no contracts. The word wife can actually be defined as woman, as God was speaking to Adam. God saw permanence, from the beginning, in spousal relationships. He rested that in concrete in Exodus 20 when He made "Adultery" an act of sin.

Basically, He meant for relationships to be with a man and a woman, and permanently. We have a nature that seeks self-satisfaction and pleasure today. Moving forward 4000 years, God further defines the steps by codifying permanent relationships by marriage. The program is defined in Ephesians 5, where marriage is pictured as exemplifying Christ and the church. The husband is to sacrifice for his spouse as Christ did for the church. The wife is to submit as "unto the Lord."   In 2021?

Since it now doesn't work out very well in 2021 with a 50% divorce rate, Paul spoke for the Lord in I Corinthians 6 & 7. It's bad enough we date multiples of the opposite sex, looking for the "right" one, which generally ends up with new dates and more breakups. Have you had more than one girlfriend, more than one spouse? He covers breakup options from God's perspective.

The comparison is that God promises to hold on to us forever. If marriage is a picture of that, then marriage in this life should also be forever. Because of God's rebellion by us, people fighting, infidelity, and just plain elongated boredom, we have today's dilemma/situation. We no longer live in a Judean/Christian culture. Society no longer guides us. Must we still state "till death do us part," or should we say "until you no longer satisfy my selfish needs or make me happy."

So if you're young and "on the verge," don't get the cart before the horse. Good sex might help, but it doesn't lead to or prolong a good marriage. Eventually, it goes away (that's why Abraham and Sarah laughed at age 75 when God said they would make a baby)(and it didn't happen for another 25 years after they laughed). Yes, God, miracles do happen.

I could go on, but it's discipline, commitment, and love (agape), that make the program work. Godspeed!

MUSIC: SALVING THE COCKLES OF ONES HEART 2021

I have a pastor friend David, who can really stroke the ivories with dexterity and GRACE. From childhood practice and young adult perfection, he can play the ol' favorites of past decades at a most enjoyable clip. The idea of sitting through modern guitar-led music for more than 2-3 iterations is, at best, tiring to my musical soul. So I guess I'm either not that musical or just plain old.

For some reason, I prefer the lyrics of Wesley, Luther, or modern Gaither, to the lyric "God is good, God is great, rah, rah, God. I also prefer, in its religious presentation, the music of Bach and Beethoven, to Hillsong, and others. But that's just me, and I don't religiously mandate that perspective to the millennial generation or generation X.

In Ephesians 5:19, we are exhorted to "addressing one another in Psalms and hymns and spiritual songs, singing and making melody to the Lord with your heart"….. So I guess it has more to do with the purpose of the music presented and not the actual music performed. Maybe the culture within which we live formulates that also in our approach. Old people "grind" through modern gatherings as the music blares, as they try to find and shut off their cell phones ringing. ☺. On the other hand, young people cringe and yawn as the fellowship meanders through "Just a closer walk with Thee."

David was known to us from the Old Testament as a music lover and talent. He played his harp and soothed the leadership in his youth. In Psalm 100, we read: "Make a joyful noise unto the Lord, all the earth." Many fellowships today, emphasize the "noise." In Psalm 101, David writes:" I will sing of steadfast love and justice to YOU oh Lord, I will make music."

So the purpose for all as Christian bodies is found in verses 20 and 21: "giving thanks always and for everything to God the Father in the name of our Lord Jesus Christ, submitting to one another out of reverence for Christ." Isn't that what it's all about? Paul seems to think so, and I guess he's God-breathed in his writings.

So keep strokin' the ivories David, and go find a room of old people. They'll love it, they'll peel forth with joyful noises, and some will cry. For a brief moment in their otherwise crusty old existences, rejected by the modern culture and sadly by family at times, they will escape to unknown zones of happiness and joy.

And you will minister to them in music, and they will minister to you in response!!!

Spirit to remember it. The evidence of that POWER is the New Testament. Can one share Jesus if they don't know Him? Of course, one can't. Must one be collegiately trained to teach others? Of course not! I think James sets the guidelines perfectly: Attitude, Lifestyle, and purity.

PS, my friend, time to get qualified! ☺

NO IRRITATIONS, NO PEARLS 2021

The oyster teaches us a great lesson. There are many examples in the bug kingdom, animal kingdom, and family kingdom that we would easily change if we could. But the lesson learned is that this life isn't a smooth existence of platitudes and success. The yellow brick (gold) road is the result of tons of material processing in this life. Our God proved that personally by His incarnation and crucifixion. One of the greatest manifestations of this is a pearl. No irritation. No pearl.

I have some talent for communicating scripture. The gift is labeled EXHORTATION. The enjoyment is watching someone "get it," "use it," and "succeed with it." I have written a number of these "1-page briefs" to that purpose. They've been flowing lately, and I love the help it seems to generate. I forgot, however, the attendant sidebar to this blessing. Fellow Christians surface to object to my concepts and focus. Family issues arise. And lastly, the more that the Spirit rises, it arouses the flesh. (Romans 7)

My point here is a beautiful pearl can only be created around an irritation. Our accuser is pictured as prowling around as a "Roaring Lion" (1 Peter 5:11). Examples throughout scripture are pictured in the lives of Abraham, Moses, David, Daniel, Jeremiah, and of course, Jesus Christ. In other words, the greater the ministry it holds, the greater the irritation. I've never been in battle, beaten, imprisoned, or thrown in a lion's den. I certainly haven't been crucified. But I have been irritated.

I just need to expect those irritations, or I can't expect the pearls. My problem is that I'm just not "trusting" A favorite author of mine, who creates daily readings, is Sarah Young. One exhortation is: "This is the way of wisdom: trusting Me (Christ) no matter what happens in your life." She always attaches scripture, and this one is Proverbs 4: 11: "I guide you in the way of wisdom and lead you along straight paths."

Do you feel led to ministry? Then get ready for the irritations! Don't duck them, but rather build off of them. Anybody who has built, or is building a successful (?) ministry will tell you about the problems which surface along the road to success. I've been creating these 1-page briefs to build people up albeit, short and sweet. The pastors of local churches don't much share the demands of boxing up a couple hundred, or a couple thousand Christians in growth mode. There's always something wrong, and they will always tell you what it is.

So accept the irritations as I struggle to do, as potential "pearls" to be created. The Patriarchs and Disciples of the Bible were never without irritations. On the contrary, they suffered measurably. "Have you considered my servant Job? Job 1:8 I don't totally get it, but it is the system within which we live. And we are the blessed who get to suffer "for His namesake." Think of pastoral irritations. Pray they become pearls. Don't let irritations bring you down. The time is short.

JUST CREATE PEARLS ☺

NO RUSH HOUR ON SUNDAY MORNING

2021

I've lived in NYC, Chicago, and Los Angeles in my life span. These cities are the Kings and Queens of rush Hour traffic tie-ups. Roads that have been constructed as super freeways, become parking lots during the morning commutes. In the late 60s, I bought a business in L.A. I was pleased to call my wife and let her know that I'd found an apartment 20 minutes from the office over the weekend. On Monday morning, I drove down to the street entrance, and traffic was backed up to that point, so I assumed there was an accident. I WAS WRONG!

It was just a normal day of commuting. I spent the next 1 ½ hours getting to the office. As a matter of fact, I spent that same time for the next 2 years before moving. I learned ways to meander from lane to lane and so I cut the time by ½ hour. I never bested that for over 3 years, and it was the worst of my travel experiences. I later commuted to the NYC area, which was similar.

We had, on occasion, the desire to travel to those cities for sporting events, plays, or church attendance. On Sunday, the freeways were empty. What a joy to traverse from Santa Clarita to Santa Monica in ½ hour. What bliss to travel from north Jersey to NYC in an hour? Without traffic, the trip was a breeze. Why? Because, "there ain't no rush hour on Sunday morning." Praise God for all the heathens.

"Remember the Sabbath to keep it Holy" Exodus 20:8. "Neglect not the gathering together as is the habit of some" Hebrews 10:25. As Christians, we are admonished to meet and greet, and take a break. Actually, God gives us a break, as He took a day of rest personally. Humans get tired after working 5-6 days, and a break for rest is a God-given repose. Society appropriated this rest centuries before. They just gradually began leaving God out of the work week, and rapidly left Him out of the rest day.

Families today have now replaced God in all facets of life, and the new rest day has been filled with sports. Children no longer need Sunday school, and it's been replaced with the little league. Families, for the most part, no longer pray together, and they, more and more, no longer stay together. Apparently, the inclination has always been there; as these verses point out, we just have new diversions.

So as a Christian, take a drive on Sunday, and thank God, who's the originator of the "rest" day. Take the first part of that day, and go worship Him, and thank Him. Take the kids to Sunday "school," where they can learn something about their Creator and how He loves them. They won't learn that in public school anymore.

Enjoy the light traffic this Sunday. Thank God again, for the rest day He initiated and passed on to us. Be thankful that we were raised in a society founded on Biblical principles because it was, even if the teachers don't know that anymore. I will guarantee you that if you take a day of rest and worship, your work days will become much more productive. God promises it! (Joshua 1:13)

I guarantee you, it will work. ☺

ON THE WINGS OF A DOVE 2021

Remember that classic song, "On the wings of a snow-white dove, He sends His pure sweet Love, a sign from above, on the wings of a dove." I can think of 2 beautiful times in biblical history when God sent a dove. The first was to Noah after months of floating aimlessly, for all he knew, on his now famous ark. In Genesis 8, we read the story of God drying off the land as God changed the atmosphere, dried the land, and settled the ark on the mountains of Ararat.

To verify it was time to disembark, Noah sent out a dove hoping it would return with vegetation, and it did. Reading chapter 8 is a real eye-opener about God's interaction in space and time. The Bible says, "God caused a wind to pass over the Earth" (Genesis 8:1). The chapter then goes into great detail on the timing of events. He ends the chapter describing ongoing seasons "while the Earth remains" That's an amazing comment/prediction. It leads me to 2 Peter 3: 10, where it states the world will be dissolved/burned up. YES, God created everything, sustains everything, and will destroy everything, before re-creating the material.

So the dove above went out to verify that at that time, new life had been created, so that Noah and his family could return to the ground, grow crops, and live on in this earthly domain. God was involved, and His messenger was this beautiful, helpless, but useful little feathered bird. God sent His message that now, all was well, and they could proceed.

God again used this beautiful little avian at Jesus' baptism by John the Baptist. John was Jesus' cousin and preached in the desert, asking people to repent and be baptized. Chapter 1 of John covers Christ's Deity fully. In verses 32-34, John states what he saw. He saw the Holy Spirit descending on Christ, "like a dove." What a beautiful and soft appellation that God the Holy Spirit rested on Christ or God the Son. John chapter 6 is a good follow-up, where Christ deals with the Trinity concept further.

So I suggest you let the wings of the dove rest on you and in you. Ask, and you will receive it, once for all, or daily, and assuredly, eternally. God's Spirit is His imputed blessing to all who believe, and receive. I don't create these "1-Page Briefs" without inspiration, motivation, and yes, guidance from my Creator. The motivation is Love (Agape'), or I'm just a noisy gong (1 Corinthians 13).

Ask today, and receive your blessing

"ON THE WINGS OF A SNOW WHITE DOVE"

OUR CREATOR, SAVIOR, and JUDGE?

JESUS CHRIST 2021

God is Love. Jesus loves you. But He's our judge? I am in a study of the book of John, and read something I hadn't noticed before. The Joy of aging is that there are always new verses to see. The Holy Spirit enlightens us, as needed, and something sticks out like it has neon lights. It's much like mining for gold. One digs and digs, and then finds a nugget. One goes through tons of dirt, seeming to take unlimited time, and then, a nugget appears, making the whole dig worthwhile.

In the book of Matthew, chapter 1, we read, "you shall call his name Jesus, for He will save His people from their sins" He is our Savior. There are multiple other references throughout the New Testament to fortify this concept and reality. He is also listed as our judge in the future, as you look at John 5. Verse 22 states: "The Father judges no one, but has given all judgment to the Son." We know this is a statement for the future eschatological existence of Christ in His heavenly Godly existence as He had stated it in His earthly existence. John 12: 47 "I did not come to judge the world, but to SAVE the world."

There are multiple scriptural locations listing our God and Savior, our Lord God, our Lord, and my God, etc., etc., etc. Basically, the God of the Bible is called God the Father, God the Son, and God the Holy Spirit. Logic tells me time was created in Genesis 1: "In the Beginning" as was man: Genesis 1:26 "Then God said, Let us make man in our Image." So it's no great thing for a student of God to see History, documentation, and future events are all in place, predicted, and timed out. Could Christ be our Creator in one age, our Savior in the current age, and our judge in the future age? Apparently, scripturally, absolutely! For those in the family, this is JOYFUL

In conclusion, then, the key in this life is to get/be saved. To be saved from what, you ask? To be saved from the judgment of the all-powerful hands of the Creator of all things. Someone rightly stated that God is LOVE, and loves all of His created beings. That's not an issue. The issue then is the rejection by us of that love in this lifetime. To miss this lifetime opportunity is tragic. Practicing sin (doing what God hates, like breaking the 10 Commandments) is what brings on death.

Have you sinned? You need to be saved! Jesus loves you! Accept that love today. Tomorrow might be too late. On the other hand, Christ will be your judge, if you have rejected His love today.

PENTECOST: THE BIG SWITCH

So what did happen to Christ's disciples? He picks a dozen ex fisherman, tax collectors, and his betrayer to follow Him, learn from Him, and believe in Him, and they scatter at His arrest, deny knowing Him, doubt His resurrection, and wonder if He was going to take over during His 40-day return. So He shoots up in the clouds as they watch, saying just prior to that it's not for them to know the dates or times, and speaks of His replacement in the entire process.

WHAT HAPPENED???

Pentecost happened, that's what. In Acts 1, Christ finishes His earthly works for the time, and is replaced by the Holy Spirit in Acts 2. The Holy Spirit arrives to fill the disciples' Spirits, and they are immediately transformed from under-educated fishermen to Scriptural scholars. Have you felt that transformation? When you read, study, and share the books written by John, Peter, and James, you realize a new power had filled their lives. Christ spoke of it, promised it, and helped fulfill it.

It was so transforming that Peter gave the momentous Pentecostal sermon, and 3000 people were saved and changed in Acts 2. As he did, the disciples joined in spreading the good news and immediately spoke in languages they had never before used, such that individuals heard and understood the Gospel message in their own tongue. God, the Holy Spirit, had arrived.

Prior to Christ's Passover, He explained the process to His followers. After His resurrection, they still didn't get it, thinking that He would wipe out Caesar and rule the world. After Pentecost, they got it. Did you get it before salvation? Did you get it before God the Holy Spirit entered and saved you? That transformation is life's greatest experience for the recipients. One passes from human nature's ignorance, to God implanted brilliance.

Do be careful, however, as it is a process. It takes time, however, an entire lifetime. It's the process of the finite learning the infinite. One can't get cocky with pride as if they have excelled over others in that process. Christ pointed out to aspiring followers, that the greatest growth as a Christian is demonstrated in greater servanthood. He showed them that with foot washing. There was no more disgusting exercise in their day than washing the dirt, grime, and smell off another's feet. The Creator of the universe stooped to that exercise for His disciples.

So we all need to make "the big switch" We each need our own Pentecost. We each need a transformation from ego-ship to servanthood. At that point, we begin the process that ends in heavenly bliss. I CAN'T WAIT for the promised, heavenly reward. We need to meet our Creator. Then we will "get" to meet HIM. ☺

DON'T BE LEFT BEHIND!

I recently saw this acronym:

PRAY

P   praise

R   repent

A   ask

Y   yield

PRAYER IN 2021   GOOGLING
GOD/INSTANTLY ACCESSIBLE

If one drives today, they probably have a cell phone. So do 90% of the rest of you. In my younger days, we had encyclopedias. Today, one just engages their cell phone. Go ahead. Ask it anything from fat calories in a hot dog to how far it is to drive to Chicago. You will be answered in seconds, at worst. You hold a mechanical device in your hand, with no strings or wires attached, and it records your touches or voice and responds instantly. Has it ever crossed your mind that the Creator of the universe has similar capabilities to hear all requests or statements at a far greater level?

If one buys into the culture that teaches that existence has evolved, this is difficult. If you accept and believe the Biblical explanation, then there is a God from which all we know was created. God deniers have come up with God alternatives since creation. Life is an accident, unborn babies aren't human, climate change is people-dependent, and death is the end of existence, probably (?).

I have a friend who works at Intel. He shared 3-4 yrs ago, that they designed a chip to perform 10MM transactions /second. 2 years later, they invented the quantum chip. The first reads a book front to back in milli-seconds. The latter just reads the book; poof. There are proofs in place that in this universe, communication speeds are now beyond comprehension. Guess what, they always were. God has the capability to process billions of prayers at a time and always has. If that weren't the case, mankind couldn't create a chip to perform similar actions. GET IT?

I grew up without computers or cell phones. When I prayed, I wondered? I read in the Bible that God actually visited people like Abraham, Jacob, Moses, David, and Solomon, to name a few. Many believers in God always prayed continually. We have a God who remains in continuous and intimate contact with His creation.

The one who struck me the most, however, was Jesus Christ. He was in continuous communication with His father from youth to the cross. He left people constantly to be alone for prayer and time with the Father. That was enough for me, but in my youth, I always wondered if my prayer got through, and as a young adult, I wondered, did my prayer get through? And now, as an old man, I know my prayers get through!

It was a great revelation, epiphany, to this experienced reprobate that the Creator of the universe, my Creator, hears, answers, saves, and communicates with me. In Revelation 8, John writes that our prayers are as incense burned before the throne of God. We get through!

So, in conclusion, I'm convinced! Having been blessed to live in this technological era, I can reach unknown computers housing untold storage of trivia. I submit that the Creator of this universe, then, is capable of hearing all, evaluating our requests, and responding to us all, just as He did since creation.

So enjoy your future prayers:

JUST GOOGLE GOD ☺

PROSPERITY FOR CHRISTIANS
HANDLING IN 2021

Much has been said of this topic in this stage of history. For the last two centuries, becoming a pastor was equivalent to taking a vow of poverty. But it's not anymore. As with a number of faith-based movements today, a dimension can be taken too far. As an example, the prosperity Gospel: is actually no Gospel at all. I believe this takes place when God's image/creation (us) takes the overzealous position for the Creator; maybe well-meaning, maybe just selfish and egotistical.

Scripture history lists many whom God has prospered for a time or lifetime. It also lists those who have had nothing. Take Abraham and the patriarchs, Joseph, Job, David, Daniel, and the richest man of all time, Solomon. When Christ came to earth, He chose to own nothing for His three years of ministry. 2nd Corinthians 8, "the grace of our Lord Jesus Christ, that though He was rich, yet for your sake, He became poor," so what then is the source of man's riches, when they exist? If we start at the very beginning, one must turn to Gen 1:1: "In the beginning, GOD created the heavens and the earth." The Genesis of life and all that exists is from the ultimate GIVER.

I then skip over to some specific scriptures that deal with the system of distribution. When dealing with His chosen people during the Exodus, God was quite specific. In Deuteronomy 28, God told the people that if they followed His rules, He would prosper them. And likewise, if they didn't follow His rules, they would be cursed. In Ecclesiastes 7, God says through Solomon, who experienced mankind's greatest personal wealth, "that He makes the good times and the poor." In Matthew 6: 35, He confirms who is really in charge of the distribution of life and wealth. I learned this when I "went broke," as they say, the first time☺. This is the source of that beautiful song, "His eye is on the sparrow."

So as a Christian, is it O.K. to be rich, relatively speaking to others? Of course, it is! Just don't take total credit or hoard it. Christ extolled the widow's mite in Mark 12. Christ also condemned the rich man who constructed more barns in His parable in Luke 12. We are given two great chapters in 2 Corinthians 8 and 9, where Paul exhorts the Corinthian church members to share their surplus. It even states that Christ, the God-Man, left total riches behind to become poor so that WE could become RICH, for "all" that "rich" means (including material wealth).

A beautiful little saint was quoted once, after spending years in a concentration death camp, that "life isn't about DURATION, but rather DONATION. Corrie Ten Boone knew the difference. This whole process of life, then, is learning about God's system of distribution. It's not about getting, it's about giving. If saved from your punishment for sin, that's all you need. From that point of knowledge, then work hard, manage your resources well, and give, give, give. And share, share, share. As the Apostle Paul stated and lived: "I have learned to be content." I heard elsewhere that being rich isn't based on what you HAVE (compared to others) but truly on what you NEED (with absolutely no comparison). Remember:

"His eye is on the sparrow, and I know He's watching you"!

"PROFESSING TO BE WISE, THEY BECAME FOOLS"   2021

I find Romans 1 to be one of the interesting, encapsulating, summarizing chapters in the entire New Testament, if not the whole Bible. Halfway through it (VS 22), Paul writes the title statement. People without God in their psyche; have exposited the texts of humanity over the ions. When they didn't know the source of creation (Genesis 1), they created evolution. When they didn't appreciate the obvious and unending benefits of fossil fuels, they invented climate change. When they didn't appreciate God, not only for creation but for sustaining creation through governments (Daniel 2, and Romans 13), they manipulated their governments as gods of power, money, and maintenance.

In the first half of this chapter, we get a heavy dose of creative theology. He tells the Romans (and us) that we can know God just by observing His creation and realizing that there had to be a Creator. He spices it up with the Gospel and the history of the Christian faith. He also covers God's other dimension of wrath toward those who "suppress the TRUTH in unrighteousness." In other words, God doesn't mess around in His Words and actions.

He then states in verse 22, "Professing to be wise, they became fools." This is nothing new for mankind. Christ notes that "in the days of Noah" (Matt 24:38), people lived without regard for their Creator, and then the Romans, to which this was written, had a society much like ours. It goes on to say, "They exchanged the truth for a lie."

The rest of the chapter then lists the collection of lifestyles and beliefs that enveloped the Roman lifestyle. It sounds like a description of our country today. The rainbow was previously a sign of God's covenant (Gen 9:13) with the world that He would never again destroy the earth with a flood. (He actually had changed the atmosphere). Today, it's the chosen symbol of the homosexual community. Check out the listed sins in the rest of the chapter. You will have no problem finding a sin or two you've experienced doing yourself.

So we can now see the dilemma within which we live. Study the Bible. Look what happens to Christian Biology teachers today if they attempt to teach

SAVED??? FROM WHAT? 2021

One of the key thoughts of Christianity is the bottom line; SALVATION. The principle is fairly simple: one needs to be saved from the consequences of breaking God's laws, i.e., the Ten Commandments. They are found in Exodus chapter 20. If you read through them, you soon realize there is no slip or slide to following God's ordained perfection. Paul states in his Galatians letter, the Law is a school teacher (Gal 3:24) to lead us to Christ. To read the Laws and consider obeying them, with our own strength and initiative, is pure folly.

Nonetheless, they make for tremendous cultural and civil mandates to run and control society. Firstly, if people really believed in their Creator, they would care about what He thinks. That is obviously not the case. Believe in Him, and trust in Him ONLY. Don't murder each other, don't steal from each other, and don't wish you had a house or vacation as nice as your neighbor. Christ added that if you hate someone, it equals murder, and if you lust after your neighbor's wife, you've committed adultery. And right in the middle of them all, it shares that you must honor your father and mother, for you snotty little ungracious kids like I was ☺.

I saw a movie a few years ago about a WW11 vet named Louis Zamperini. He was an Olympic athlete and bomber pilot, and his plane was shot down in the pacific. He floated for 47 days living off of rainwater and fish and birds he could catch. He was then captured and spent two years under Japanese internment, torture, and beatings. He returned to L.A. and sadly became a drunk. He knew what it meant to be saved from his ocean experience. He was walking down the streets of Hollywood soon after and went into a Billy Graham crusade in L.A. HE GOT SAVED again, but differently! He knew what it was to be lost, and need saving. He got it, and spent the last third of his life appreciating it and sharing his story.

Have you hit bottom yet?

I didn't have to go that far. I got saved as a young lad. I didn't hit bottom before I got saved but in the "middle." Everyone's different! But I do know what I have been saved from. In James 2:10, we lose all our wiggle room. What's noteworthy in the book written by James, Scripture says that by breaking one, we're guilty of all. You mean I'm as guilty as a murderer or thief if I dishonor my parents? That was a problem I had to work out personally. I finally realized that my parents did the best they could with what they had to work. I asked for their forgiveness. Thank God that we're saved!

Saved from what, then? Saved from sin; that's what! What sin? It's when you break your Creator's perfect rules and regulations. That's why the Bible teaches we need a sacrificial lamb, a savior. "You will call Him Jesus, because He will save them from their sins" (Matt 1:21). It's what the Bible is all about. It's a lifebuoy that you can grab hold of.

Grab it today! You might not make it 47 days……..like Louie did.

SEEN GOD LATELY? 2021

As I approach this topic, I'm reminded I have 7 senses (Google them). I'm either trapped by them, or appreciate the full availability in my body for their use. Pastor Jon's lead-in for his study of John is John 1:18: "no one has seen God." The 1st chapter shows that Jesus is God, made manifest, and reveals God's reality in the flesh (verse 14). This is all spoken to allay the confused who can't accept verse 1. "In the beginning was the Word, and the Word was with God, and the Word "WAS" God. Is this a part of the "mystery of Christ" pastor Darryl taught us in Ephesians 3? Does God keep mysteries for us?   Proverbs 25:2. "It is the glory of God to conceal a matter." Jon might have added, "John" who quoted Jesus in John 6:46, "Not that any man has seen the "FATHER," except the one who is from God, He has seen the father"…

But my question to Professor Dave was, hadn't Abraham, Moses, Jacob. Solomon and Daniel seen Him? It was a huge occasion to see the almighty at any age. What a privilege to walk with God as the disciples did, or meet Him on the Damascus road as Paul did. So what was Christ referring to? I believe I may have had an epiphany in writing this brief. As I pass this on to my scholarly pastors, I can assure you that if incorrect, I will be skewered. ☺ ☹

So Jesus had an encounter with a Samaritan woman in John 4. For the Jews, that was akin to sharing with a Las Vegas prostitute. Jesus said you Samaritans got it all wrong and that salvation is from the Jews. She replied that the Messiah was coming to explain all, and He answered, I am here now, so listen! And right in the middle of that explanation, Christ said, "God is Spirit." Just what did He mean? In the 1st chapter, He already explained He is God, revealing God, explaining God, and sitting at the right hand of God. Getting confused? I have been!

And then I thought, can the created human mind see a spirit? Is it another dimension needing perception and exposure? I watch America's Got Talent on TV and enjoy the magicians. They perform impossible illusions that only they know. I think it's like the magicians Moses met at his encounter with Pharaoh. These TV tricks almost seem demonic in terms of impossible actions to mind reading activities.

So may I conclude that God can't be seen because He's a Spirit? Is it an option without a deep dive into charisma? Could He have appeared in "the garden," a burning bush, wrestled Jacob, gone for a weenie roast in the furnace, or showed up for Jesus' baptism? If God is Spirit, what are the limits? I propose; NONE!

When Moses asked for a name and ID, God said, "I AM who I AM" (Exodus 3:14). When Christ got in His daily tussle with the Jewish religious leaders, He said, "before Abraham was born, I AM" (John 8:58), and they knew what He meant, and went forward to crucify the blasphemer (in their minds). John 8 is a cool chapter and worth the re-read. Be careful when you criticize; the gun may be facing you as you self-righteously pull the trigger.

So is it possible? I haven't seen God because "in Spirit," He can't be seen by created humans. People have seen Christ and felt and been led by the Holy Spirit. By the words of John 1, Christ is God. We learn in Acts 5 that the Holy Spirit is God. Take it to your Spiritual bank.

We "created" humans, know who God is by His testimony. Beginning in Genesis 1:1, "In the beginning, God created the heavens and the universe" (and us). "For since the creation of the world, God's "INVISIBLE" qualities…have been clearly seen (Romans 1:20). So then, we actually see the manifestations of God through the creation and the SON.

But as Jesus stated, no created being has seen God the Father, or God the Spirit. Don't let it bother you true-believer, that's changing soon.

BET YOUR LIFE ON IT ! ☺

SET YOUR MINDS ON THE THINGS
ABOVE, Colossians 3, 2021

I think, at this point in life, Colossians 3 is one of the best texts I've read on how to get through this life. How does one handle conflicts, people situations, marriage, family, and work? The barrage is constant, and if I'm correct," till death do us part"☺. We are admonished, commanded, and encouraged at the beginning to follow this "briefs" title. I share with a pastor/friend whose calendar is full of members/attendees at our church who can't handle the problems of life. It's never-ending!

In further verses, we are admonished that those of different heritage, life position, or gender, are to be loved and not powered over or discriminated against. If not, we prove to be the foolish creations that the WORD describes prolifically. We are to "forgive as the Lord forgave you" (did you get that?). History and societies seem to reflect God's judgment toward Eve in Genesis, where God deals out pain in childbirth, and women being ruled by their husbands. Has that changed around the world?

Since Paul wrote about the clothing (ver 12) we are to wear, dress up! He goes on to say:"Let the WORD of Christ dwell in you richly." How's that going? This, then, leads us to those grinding, daily, meat-on-the-bone statements about family members getting along. The 5th commandment commands us to "honor our father and mother." (even if you don't like them anymore). Take your parents out of your life, as an example. What experience and blessings did you just erase? Hmmm, we may need to think this over, and you might include birth (or your creation) as well.

I believe that's the whole point moving ahead in verses 18+. After 8 decades, I can assure you family is where the rubber meets the road, and the joys and blessings of life are under shadowed by the "other stuff that goes with it. Enough said, but my Pastor/Friends calendar is still full next week. I've deduced that life is but a reflection, pointed out in this text, of our attitude toward God. 3 verses leaped out at me as I studied this: 22, "reverence for the Lord," 23, "working for the Lord," and 24, "it is the Lord Christ you are serving."

Get it? Your attitudes and actions in life are then simply a reflection of your attitudes and actions with or toward your Creator. Husbands, have you been

154

harsh? Women, can't submit? Children, can't obey? Dads, do kids drive you nuts? Can't stand your boss? Can't handle your employees? Let's jump to our God relationship. How's the reverence going? Who are you really reporting to, and are you truly serving Christ in all that you do? Or, in the process, have you just replaced God in asking them to obey, respond, and serve you in the process?

I wish I'd truly "GOT" this 50 years ago. I can't say life would have been any easier, but it is a far better management program. When one applies the Creator's management system, it seems that the elements of family and society would function much better. Give it a shot! You now have a focused outline for success. Aim higher this time. We might be able to free up some extra time for my Pastor/friend ☺

SHARING THE GOSPEL: MORMONISM
2021

A good start might just be the Gospel: (1 Corinthians 15:1-4), "want to remind you of the Gospel,,, "Christ died,,, was buried,,, was raised on the 3rd day,,, according to the Scriptures." The first aim of all other-Biblical/Christian sects/cults is to attack the Deity of Christ as stated in Scripture. "They went out from us, but they didn't really belong to us" (1 John 2:19). This is due to the Bible's original authorship by God versus the devil and his antichrist teachings. John 1: "In the beginning was the Word, and the Word was God."

My attitude in sharing is soft and God-Loving. My goal is to share "full of Grace, and seasoned with salt." I don't wish to be harsh or contentious in this brief (Colossians 4:5, 6). In "Passport to Heaven," Micah Wilder (an ex-Mormon missionary) shares his conversion as he tried to convert a Baptist minister. In chapters 9-11, he details that experience and the eventual outcome. The reality is that most Christians don't have that much gunpowder in their artillery and many times shoot blanks. Fortunately, Ephesians 2: 8, 9 is a sufficient explanation.

This Mormon faith group emerged in the early 1800s when a self-proclaimed prophet took the stage. He proclaimed visions (unproven), and wrote the book of Mormon. Not one scintilla of evidence exists to support the claims of this book. The Bible, however, has been verified by non-Biblical writings, and archeology, in great depth. The book of Mormon, then, must be considered a book of fantasy, created by this self-called prophet, never verified to be non-fiction in any scholarly fashion. Joseph Smith also spoke of Christianity being dead since written. The Bible was incorrect in its versions, according to him, to the point he rewrote the Old Testament to correct the errors. Mormon bishops will corroborate that fact. What he didn't see coming were the "Dead Sea Scrolls" in 1948, which confirmed the veracity of the old testament of 1830, and he sadly continued the falsehood that Jesus came again to North America to preach the Mormon gospel.

The reality of the Bible is that "the Word became flesh" (John 1 14) and that Jesus is the "Son of God," not one of a progressive list of sons of god. The great miracle message of the NT is just that. It is well covered in Colossians creation theories instead of evolution. What happens to history teachers who read the "Declaration of Independence" where it states we are endowed "by our Creator" with Life, Liberty, and the pursuit of happiness? Don't even try to equate abortion with murder unless you crave your pink slip.

So we see today how we've paralleled the Romans Paul addressed his letter to. We're recycling history instead of improving it. I write this for the sake of my grandchildren, if they have ears. Society is no longer a teacher/influencer for upcoming generations. There are a lot of positives in this passage if you join the winning team. The competition is tough, aggressive, and determined, and it doesn't take opposition lightly. They wish to suck you into their ultimate failure in the future,

As Joshua said in Joshua 24:15, "choose this day who you will serve," and don't wait too long. Don't push God's patience and mercy too far. Read and re-read Romans 1. You'll be blessed and educated. ☺

1: 15-18. Christ didn't "just" pre-exist, He always existed. We were created (Jeremiah 1:5). It is obvious to the reader, then, that Mormonism is indeed "another gospel' (Galatians 1:8 and 9). We are forced to be candid that one must accept some lies perpetrated by LDS religious leaders, not the least of which is eternal marriage disclaimed by Christ Himself (Matthew 22:30), to be a member of that religion.

A totally human thought came to mind, "you can't fight stupid." Have you tried to argue creation against evolution lately? The die, for this cast, seems to have been set for the 21st century. When "non-believers" in anything (especially the God of creation) (Genesis 1:1) are exposed to the truth as espoused in the scripture, Mormons are generally stuck in concrete. But for Grace, my fellow Christians, we ourselves would still be there! ☹ We must keep presenting as we are prepared "for the work of the ministry" (Eph 4). As I previously said to my sales teams, "you always give your "sales prospects" an opportunity to say yes, even if the majority of contacts say no."

YOU MIGHT JUST GET A YES ☺

SHARING THE GOSPEL #2 2021

I attended a concert by "Adams Road" this weekend. This group of ex-Mormons converted to Christianity, which was a blessing and an education. I loved the t-shirts emblazoned with "JESUS IS ENOUGH," although I wasn't all that excited about the small pink shirt that I won during the knowledge contest about Micah's conversion. (I'm 6'2" and 250#s).

I picked up 2 very critical enjoyments from their testimonies: 1)3 steps to consider for sharing my faith, and 2) a new song for my blessed list. The 3 steps I wrote down were:

1) The Cross is foolishness to those perishing (1 Corinthians 18)
2) We are saved by Grace(Eph 2:8,9),
3) Read the New Testament like a child (also my brief on the 10 basic chapters)

So I thought, make sure you get to know your customer; listen. It's just old sales parlance applied to sharing the faith. Different product, same process. We learn at some point that no Holy Spirit, no comprendo. Paul mentions that later in (1 Cor 2:16), "We have the Mind of Christ" It just happens that we're involved in that process with our sharing.

Secondly: Saved by Grace (Eph 2:8,9) "For by Grace you have been saved through faith, and that not of yourselves, it is the gift of God." You can put pride of accomplishment, closing skills, and powers of persuasion to rest. Nothing happens if you remain silent, but nothing also happens without God the Holy Spirit activating one's SOUL.

Thirdly, start reading scripture. I loved what Micah said, however, to read it like a child. The first 3 chapters of John are amazing. Don't study it, discern it, and get commentaries, etc.; just read it three times like a child.

Micah, or Joseph, mentioned these 3 in their testimonies. It takes all the pressure of rejection off the table. As an old sales manager, I love that thought. As I motivated past sales teams, "just give them a chance to say yes." Don't pass on a chance! You never know. I asked the obvious question in a small home Bible study once, and a lone attendee said yes. I almost replied out loud, "REALLY"? That person got saved that night. WOW!

A last thought from Micah as he left the religion in which he was raised, that destroys who Christ is (GOD), and what Jesus' life was about:

Jesus isn't just a part of my testimony; HE "IS" MY TESTIMONY.

And that led to the climax: they sang a song they wrote named "Son of Man" In that song is a verse saying Christ saw my face when on His cross. I believe that! The God I now know is the God of the complete universe and quantum chips, for example. He has no current limitations (He is Spirit), and His potential is unfathomable. I now will tie this to a couple other favorites, "I can Only Imagine" and "Amazing Grace."

"God bless you having been saved forever as you "work out your salvation, for it is God who is at work in you." Philippians 2:12, 13

SIN PACKAGES: WHAT'S YOURS? 2021

The oldest question a kid ever says to their parent is, "What did I do"? Most of the time they already know, but sometimes it's a valid approach. Part of the learning process is simply to codify the old list of what's right, and what's wrong. We hire counselors as we age, to figure out what we're doing wrong, and how to escape the results of these "sins." Did you ever get pulled over and asked the officer, "What did I do"? Relax, sin actually means to miss the mark. It may be a bad school situation, a family situation, or even a legal situation.

The amazing fact is that God gave us a set of Commandments to live by, that sums up the positives and negatives. Christ summed it up by saying, "Love God with all your heart, mind, and soul, and love your neighbor as yourself." He went on to define your neighbor in the parable of the Good Samaritan. If you were a Jew at that time, you knew there was no such thing as a Good Samaritan. In Galatians 3:24, then, we read that we can't really "keep" the 10 Commandments, and their real purpose is to lead us to faith in our Creator for repentance and forgiveness.

I submit for some breakdown that we "tend" to break some but not others. It makes no difference to God as we read in James 2:10 that if we break one, we're guilty of all. Wow, if I sass my mom, I'm as guilty as if I'd murdered? That's a high standard; perfection. Maybe now you'll better appreciate Jesus Christ going to the cross for YOUR sins. Some people cuss God's name. Some people skip church, some lust, and some lie. When you turn your back on Jesus, what do you tend to do? There was a period when I dishonored my parents, I have a tendency to lust (now that I'm old, that's kind of silly), and I can sprinkle in some covetousness.

What tugs on your shirttails when you aren't exercising faith? A little cussing of Jesus' name? Do you skip church fellowship? Are you jealous of your neighbor's riches, lifestyle, or wife? I think you can get the point here. There is a constant tug by the old sinful nature (your personality). The beauty of salvation in this life, is the alternative to that thinking, by yielding to the Holy Spirit for guidance and satisfaction. At some point later in life, you will be approaching the end. You can't offset Spiritual thinking with activities, trips, or saliencies in human activity.

So check out the big ten. See if you can identify the "big three" that might plague or irritate you. Focus on faith and prayer, and allow the packages to fade. Start early in life, as the payoff at the end is marvelous (Revelation 21, 22).

The best/worst case scenario is you will at least be aware of what to run to:

and from what to run away!

STRENGTH FROM ADVERSITY 2021

I could have said strength "in" adversity, but it comes with the process. I've heard of great ministries that came through their "red Seas," or desert, and were tipped into thinking when I heard Rick Warren share how significant ministries seem to follow tragedy. In his case, his son committed suicide at age 27. Rick Warren went on to lead congregants to share the gospel in 200 countries, and write the best-selling non-fiction Christian book in history other than the Bible.

I enjoy a daily reading (Jesus Calling) by Sarah Young with Jesus' guidance and attendant Bible verses every day. She suffered miserably for a year with Lyme disease only to emerge with Christian sharings that she fully credits to her sufferings. Joni Erickson Tada has suffered a lifetime of pain and sleeplessness while creating and sustaining a magnificent ministry for people in wheelchairs.

Then there's little ol' me. About 3 ½ yrs ago, I suffered a stroke. I couldn't walk, and my left arm was limp. I wasn't sure of the future at age 75, but I only focused on the present enough to exercise my way back to mobility. I guess the most significant change was riding a 3-wheel bike, and driving my car again. I'm not sure if all that gave me the focus to create my "1-page briefs" or not, but it is most humbling to live through a period of helplessness.

Have you considered the Oyster, dear reader? Without a major irritation, it has a worthless life. Well, maybe a bite-sized meal for one's fancified appetizer. The oyster produces one of life's glorious beauties, short of a hardened crystal or gold. The best of the best are draped around the necks of the more wealthy as a sign of opulence. Its creation is due to irritation. As minuscule sand lodges in the oyster, secretions salve the pain, and a beautiful pearl is formed.

What are the pearls in your life? What were the irritations? My main irritation was the struggle to overcome a debilitating stroke. The pearls, I believe, have been my short briefs. I create them, love the messages, and they seem to bless some friends, and the creations (maybe irritations) continue. ☺

BEAUTIFY YOUR IRRITATION; TODAY ☺

This, then, is a beautiful time of the year. When we lived in the N.E., as the trees shed their leaves, that annual death scene was marvelous with the reds, and yellows, and purples. As a golfer, I enjoyed them even more since the fairways cut through rows of beautiful old trees, from elm to maple. In Colorado, we enjoyed the annual death of the millions of Aspen tree leaves. God's annual program was a beautiful thing to observe.

So let me encourage you this season. Be thankful! In everything, for everything, because of everything.

Thankfulness is a gift from God. ☺

THE END IS HERE (2021)

To some, that sounds gloomy, while others are joyous. I love Titus 2:13,14: "waiting for our blessed hope, the appearing of the Glory of our great God and Savior Jesus Christ, who gave Himself for us to redeem us from all lawlessness and to purify for Himself a people for His own possession who are zealous for good works." I share Paul's excitement

A key event mentioned about the "end times" is the "rapture" (taking away). As a Christian, one doesn't argue about the 'whether' of this event in the future, but the 'when'. Nobody can argue about the 7 years of God's judgment for the earth, but again, the when. The rapture is mentioned specifically in 1st Thessalonians 4. I think the "focus" on this tribulation period of time should/must be, for whom is this judgment set in place? As Christians are judged in Christ, there is no further God-judgment necessary for the Redeemed.

Biblically, the removal of the saints before God's judgment is exemplified in Noah, Lot, Elijah, Enoch, and the 2 witnesses in Revelation. Of course, Jesus Christ was raptured in Acts one. A book for all the different positions on Bible Prophecy was written by Dr. Ron Rhodes, "The 8 great Debates of Bible Prophecy." He is a graduate of Dallas Seminary and shares positions of some notables like John MacArthur, Hal Lindsey, Tim Lahaye, David Jeremiah, and many more. The paperback, however, includes all disciplines of end times thinking and is well written for a simple understanding of these very important conclusions. I have known Born-Again Christians who have different positions on end-time events, but all are unanimous on the necessity of believing the GOSPEL, detailed in 1 Corinthians 15.

We, therefore, take a position that the judgment is not destined for born-again believers who have trusted in Christ, His forgiveness, and His substitutionary death and punishment for our sins. This leads logically to a PRE-TRIB timing for the Rapture. Christians will be removed from the earth so God can unleash His judgment on unbelief. In reading Revelation 6, we see terrible events up to and including ¼ of all people being killed. When God judged Sodom and Gomorra, He wouldn't do it until Lot, and his family left town. God then burned it down.

The 2nd main event, then, is the physical return of our Christ at the end of this 7-year judgment to end the Armageddon battle, with His "feet" landing on the Mt of Olives, and His 1000-year reign on earth, WITH US, from Jerusalem. So the lasting picture, then, of the final end events is a Rapture, a 7-year judgment, the physical return of Jesus Christ to earth this time, and His 1000-year reign. (Revelation 20)

In conclusion, prophecy clarifies as it fulfills. No one argues today that Christ's birth in Bethlehem was foretold! There are numerous other examples of fulfilled prophecy. Even though modern experience has shown the weakness of many badly speculated end-time positions, people who are cemented into various conclusions just can't let go, even with logical proof.

The fact is, in Scripture, Christ will return, in the air, to receive trusting believers, just as a farmer completes his harvesting. The fact is, He will return again in 7 years, with us, and His (Jehovah/Jesus) feet will land in Israel. (Zach 14)

<<<I CAN'T WAIT ☺>>>

THE END IS HERE #2 2021

Current events drive the title of this brief. As we observe, not celebrate, the 20th anniversary of 9/11, we are warned in a Jonathan Cahn book called "The Harbinger" that this was an act allowed by God to warn the United States that sin in society was rising to the point of judgment. I agree. Ironically, but not coincidental, the World Trade Center was constructed on the same garden churchyard where George Washington and the first USA Congress had kneeled to pray for our country's dedication and salvation.

And as I pen this brief, our most populated and 3rd physically sized state in the US, has voted by a 2/3 majority to maintain a system that denies creation by God (Genesis 1), promotes murdering unborn children (Jeremiah 1:5), and supports homosexual and unbridled sex (Romans 1: 18-32). It's most interesting to me that these are in direct opposition to the Bible.

Now I appreciate that over 80% of the populated world could care less about what the Bible has to say. Born Again Christians, however, have learned over time that the veracity of scripture is something one can hang their hat on, so to speak, and indeed their whole existence; past, present, and future. Solomon certainly claimed that as he stated that without God and His guidance, life was futile and meaningless. If you haven't read up on Solomon, he made Gates, Musk, Bezos, and the modern-day billionaires, look like piker's.

Remember when the religious and political leadership came after Jesus Christ? We now know by faith and scripture that they were blind in their pursuit. It's an amazing blessing to have one's eyes opened to our Creator and sustainer. It's hard to believe that so many of God's creations have been blinded by the truth. It's incredible for those of us blessed with this sight and insight, to realize what God, through Christ, has done for us, and through us.

So today, one of the largest States in the un-United States has voted to slam the door on the Bible. It has voted to go against the mandates of scripture and live in and for sin. Is this the future of our country? 50 years ago, my wife and I started in this beautiful State. At least 3 great ministries began back then, including John MacArthur, Rick Warren, and Hal Lindsey. Bible schools started or existed like Biola, Master's College and Seminary, and

Fuller Seminary. To me, these were roses blooming in the desert. Today, they are blossoms on a dung heap.

I wouldn't tell anyone to quit and run for cover. I think of my grandchildren: keep your nose to the grindstone, keep reading, keep growing, prosper in what you do, share with the people in need, but grow in Christ! That's what Ecclesiastes is all about. If you pursue success in life without God, Solomon states it is meaningless. Read the "turn, turn, turns" in chapter 3. Be successful without your Creator, and the benefits accrue to those left behind, not you. Thank God for all you receive, for where you live, and for whoever joins you in your pursuit.

Our society and culture is certainly nearing its end, just as other Godless cultures over the past 6 millennia, but for me and you,

IT'S JUST BEGINNING!

THE FINAL JUDGEMENT AND
EXHORTATION   2021

My Wed pastor Jeff shared the chapter of Revelation 18 last week. Rev 18 is a sad expose, of the final judgment of God on our world system. Do you doubt that God will finally get so upset that He can no longer allow a sinful world to ignore His Love and patience (mercy). How many more unborn babies can He allow to be destroyed? How much more of the Romans 1 list will He abide? Will it happen? Ask the people who lived when Noah built God's ark, and the door shut. Ask the Egyptians who lived at the time Moses gave Pharaoh a visit. Ask the people of Sodom and Gomorrah when Lot left town. God has proven that He has limits.

In this future cataclysmic time project, it appears that distribution ceases. No water, no food, no jewelry (the loss of gold and silver and hoarding wealth), and no supplies for building. Lastly, it states that famine, plagues, and fires will take place. WOW, that sounds like I'm watching Fox news today. As stated, it speaks of luxury and splendor ending. We have significant splendor today from Las Vegas to NYC, to Cruise ships, and so forth. It visualizes sea captains seeing this great city depicted as Babylon, going up in flames. No matter the details of reality, the system will fail and die and be destroyed, just like Sodom, Egypt, and Noah-ville. ☹

However, the teacher focused on the 20th verse, which leaped out to me in the Spirit: "Rejoice over her, oh Heaven, and you saints and apostles and prophets, for God has given judgment FOR YOU against her." JUSTICE is served! And we get to watch it! Now, I'm not really "jumping up and down happy" about this, but it seems that the spectator seats are definitely pleasured by the events. Focus on this, my readers; God is LOVE (1 John 4:16), God is merciful (Deuteronomy 4:31), but; God is just (Rev 18:20).

He closes this foreboding chapter with the "NO MORES": no more Babylon. No more harpists (music), no more craftsmen, no more mills (food processing), no more lights, and no more marriage. It seems that all we enjoy (have enjoyed) in this life will cease! He speaks of tossing a giant stone into the sea. Present-day eschatologists' argue this to be literal or figurative. At the infamous JPL (Jet Propulsion Lab), they have projected a giant asteroid to pass by in 2029. Coincidence??? Biblically, this event is set in time at the mid-tribulation point of prophecy.

At any rate, we are promised the final end to the World's economic, political, and power systems, where God's justice is enacted, once and for all! Consider over history how great powers have come and gone. Read the curses listed in Old Testament Ezekiel. Where is Egypt, Persia, Greece, or Rome today? These once world powers are today's also-rans. As a Biblicist, the future history is as solid as the past. Why? Because the Bible reveals, the author (GOD) is the Creator and sustainer of all life, past, present, and future. Join me in this revelation concerning God the Creator and sustainer. Join me in this leap of faith as to who actively: made it happen, keeps it happening, and will soon end it; the existence, as we know today.

Doom and gloom? Not in the least! Be a rejoicer, as chapter 20 encourages/admonishes. Only one team wins the Super Bowl, World Series, or Final 4. Be a part of that team. But do get in the stands for that final game and REJOICE! The Bible just asks one to receive (John 1:12).

Have you taken that step? Take that step! You won't regret it, for sure! ☺

THE JESUS VACCINE 2021

As we live through the pandemic year of 2021, one can observe/experience the oppressions of mankind to one another. As extreme as that sentence seems, recent history has witnessed the tyranny of the wicked in countries such as Germany, Cuba, Venezuela, and of course, China. When Godless people are at the helm, so to speak, the people suffer and die to ruthless leadership. It happened in Noah's day, Jeremiah's day, and definitely Christ's day. And today???

I never dreamed in my 8 decades that I would see the government of the United States succumb to Godless leadership, but we've arrived. It's amazing to me that our Congress still has a Chaplin, as they pass laws to squander our wealth, ignore natural God-given resources, deny the creation by God, take credit from our Creator for changes in weather, and murder our unborn babies.

What does this all lead to in a nation of people gradually and now aggressively giving up on the principles upon which our nation was founded? We started by saying that we were "endowed by our Creator with life, liberty, and the pursuit of happiness." Today, our current administration would have us believe it comes from them.

Remember the famines of Genesis 41 and 42 that God took credit for? And what of the 10 spies other than Joshua and Caleb, who gave the Israelites a bad report so that God killed them with a plague? I would have you consider Christ's prediction in Matthew 24 of famines and earthquakes. So when God is ready to warn His creation, the sky is literally the limit. He has (and I could list many more if this wasn't a 1-page brief) sent natural calamities, and famines, and plagues, and PANDEMICS. And God doesn't need a Dr. Fauci to try and create man-designed vaccines to save the universe.

May I suggest that what society needs in the present, as well as the last 2000 years, is the JESUS VACCINE. The fear of this latest God-ordained pandemic is one's death. People will do anything to live another 10 years. If one isn't afraid to die, as they read John 3:16, it's not a worry. These vaccines are available every Sunday at Born-Again churches, where loving Christians gather to be taught and to fellowship. The vaccinations are free, and they come in a cup. Attitude and repentance is the key to successful inoculation, but the guarantee of ETERNAL life is written on the label.

Have you been putting off a vaccination as you can't decide which one to use? Do you wish for an experimental drug, or would you prefer a tried and tested, researched and resolved formula for success?

Don't wait!!! Get vaccinated this weekend ☺

THE TRINITY 2021: What have I learned? My union with Christ and the benefits

My focus has been on seeking a greater understanding of just who God is, or as Paul stated in Philippians 3: "the surpassing worth of knowing Christ Jesus my Lord," and further: "I want to know Christ." With that in mind, I was led to the reality of the Trinity in scripture. I was set back a bit by Macarther and Mayhue stating, "Since the Trinity cannot be comprehended by the human mind," that I was possibly climbing a rope covered with grease. Nonetheless, I pursued the subject.

Who is God? He is called Creator, Father, Son, and Holy Spirit. I will try and filter the scriptural facts through my finite brain and logic. Gen 1 refers to God the Creator. Deuteronomy 6: "the Lord is one." Again in Gen 1, we read: "Let us (plural) make mankind in our image." John 5 notes the reference to Christ as the Son of God, making Him EQUAL with God. In Acts 5, the Holy Spirit is referred to as being lied to, and Ananias and Safire lying to God.

One other element to this God/Creator discussion is the concept of infinity. The Bible begins the saga of life with "in the Beginning." God was already there before life was activated. He is eternal; past, present, future. "Before Abraham was, I AM." God spoke this to Moses in Exodus 3, and Christ spoke this in John 8. We were then created into this forever existence at a point in time by an infinite God Being; Praise the Lord!

Not just a few theologians have attempted to explain these definitions/perspectives/views etc., of just who God is. What sets this Godhead apart from human Creation? My observation is the" lack of conflict." They agree on everything. Are there any two created humans who don't eventually disagree on something? As Henny Youngman used to joke, "Take my spouse, please!" (Speaking in reference to opinions) Spouses fight, neighbors fight, churches fight, and so do countries. The final world conflagration will involve the greatest world powers with "blood to the bridles" (Revelation 14)

So, I'll try not to complicate the subject anymore. God is ONE! And yet operates as three different entities. He's definitely one unified being but separated in operation. The reason I know He is one, is due to the fact of total agreement, working together for mutual goals of accomplishment. Each has a role, like when Jesus and the Holy Spirit traded places in Acts 2. Peter went from a dumb-downed liar to a brilliant scholar and author of his epistles. R.C. Sproul points out that Romans 1 covers the subject well for us while at the same time pointing out that "our fallen natures do not want us to believe in God."

The benefit(s) as I see it then is the ability to live in harmony, potentially now, with fellow Christians, or just other created humans, based on appropriating His Godly Spirit. It doesn't demand change from others, but an internal transformation of my thoughts and reactions. This can be manifested in a "foot washing" attitude. I hope to change from a selfish set of needs, to a selfless level of thinking.

The Trinity is my example; three personalities serving one purpose Inscrutable for a created human, I think, but God has imputed His Spirit into me. I need to rely on/submit to Him. Who is God? I think the Athanasius Creed covers it; inscrutable for this sinner, but open to research, learning, application, and fulfillment in this life, but so enjoyable in the world to come for those who take the leap of faith.

THREE THINGS PEOPLE HATE 2021

You might be saying, "is that all"? Just three? I try to keep things short and sweet (?) in these briefs, and I seem focused on these basics. People, in general, hate to consider "Depression, War, and Death." Not everyone, but most, experience the first two, but all experience the last one. And yet it seems everyone avoids the topics unless they are forced into them.

The generation before mine experienced all three. I was born in the early 40s, so my parents were born before WW1, and lived through WW2, as well as the Great Depression, and, of course, passed on. Since schools seemed to have begun de-emphasizing history, or worse, rewriting it, the cyclical dimension of history is lost to the young. Every 100 years, we have had wars, depressions, and death. Why don't we (mankind) see the repetition and plan for it?

Firstly, let us consider Depression. I mean here, "to go broke," as they say. I don't mean a state of mind we all experience to one degree or another; some to the extreme of self-inflicted death. Yes, people go broke. I have lost businesses, missed house payments, or spent beyond my means to pay over the years. Back in the 1930s, our whole country saw a floundering, failing economy. This was exacerbated by a God-ordained drought in the vast mid-western grain fields.

Everyone loves it when the economy and life renders us "healthy, wealthy, and wise." The inescapable fact is that God sends us droughts. Why? To demonstrate God's ultimate power over nature, as opposed to ours. The latest creation of the ungodly is climate change. The latest spin is that pollution, created by God-given fossil fuels, can be controlled by mankind. It didn't work in Old Testament history, and it won't today.

The second is War. From the time of Abraham, Moses, and Joshua, mankind has fought over turf ownership. In our own wonderful country, we fought for our origins and freedom, we fought amongst ourselves in the massive and ugly civil war, and as we passed through the World Wars and Vietnam, and we're still at it today, from Afghanistan to Israel to our own borders. We hate it, but "IT" continues.

Lastly, most hate to consider DEATH. As a Biblical Christian, I am totally excited by the subject. I'm not excited about the process, just the end game.

For those who realize they were created and have "repented" in Spirit to the rules they have broken, as set by their Creator, there is the magnificent promise of life, thereafter, forever, and blessed by existence in heaven. Call it fantasy for an unknown future, but it's highlighted over and over in Scripture and preached by the world's Savior Himself, Jesus Christ.

The third topic, then, Death, confirms the rejection of God's love message, and His Word (the Bible), and these are destined for eternal separation and destruction, so, of course, they don't wish to sit around and discuss the topic. I got an "advanced" education for my perceived and proven success in my economic life. I "worked out, ran, and lifted weights" for my perceived and proven athletic successes. I read the Bible to gain a picture of the future.

I look forward to that promised future! ☺

TILL DEATH DO US PART 2021

The two most significant elements of anyone's life are the moment of birth and the moment of death. As one grows in stature, maturity, and as life lengthens, the biggest question becomes, "where will I be after I die"? For the Christian, there is no question at all. For the non-believer, there is nothing but questions.

For a Bible believer, we see mankind's representative (Adam) set our program right from the beginning. God has said repeatedly that He loves us, "BUT." As the story goes, Adam started out by doing something God didn't want him to; as it is written, "You may surely eat of every tree of the garden, but of the tree of knowledge of good and evil, you shall not eat, for, in the day that you eat of it, you shall surely die." And so, death entered into man's existence.

From then until the great flood of Noah's time, man lived for hundreds of years. But they then passed on. God changed the atmosphere, and life shortened to 70 or 80 years (Psalm 90:10). If you don't believe scripture, ask an insurance agent. They make $BB's on that fact.

So what does the Bible have to say on perpetual existence, then? In Daniel 12:2: "and many of those who sleep in the dust of the earth, shall AWAKE, some to everlasting life and some to shame and everlasting contempt" (share with a JW acquaintance). Jesus Christ said He was going to prepare a place for His followers and believers. John 14. In 1 John 5:13, we read: "I write these things to you who believe in the name of the Son of God that you may know that you have eternal life."

On the other side, people reject God ☹. It's no joke, my friend. If you reject the love of your Creator, who went so far as to sacrifice His only begotten Son, are you expecting Nirvana? In Revelation 20:15, we read: "And if anyone's name was not found written in the Book of Life, he/ (she) was thrown into the lake of fire. Christ spoke of a place to His disciples: "where their worm does not die, and the fire is not quenched." I don't want to be there for a moment, let alone eternity!

So the Bible is explicit. We are born (created), live our life, and die (cease to exist in this life). But Christ came to say that we need to be born again. It's all explained in John 3. We are not to be born over in the flesh, but we have an internal Spirit that has to be made alive by our God, the Holy Spirit. Statistics verify that this only takes place in less than 15-20% of all people. One becomes born-again, and KNOWS when it happens. They also start bearing fruit just as grapes grow on the vine, and oranges on a tree. But that's another subject.

So if you want the benefits, get in the program. Be sorry (called repenting) to your Creator, accept His forgiveness, and you're in. There's a room/mansion waiting for you.

NO WORMS ATTACHED!

TRUST AND BE JOYFUL 2021

After 75 or 80 "1 Page Briefs," this is a nice interlude. Take a break! Give it a breather. Re-oxygenate.

So I was reading my daily devotional the past week and ran into this suggested break. Trust in me forever, for I am the ROCK eternal. This exhortation is from Isaiah 26:4 "Trust in the Lord, for the Lord is the Rock Eternal." Be joyful in hope. Romans 12:12. Be joyful in hope, patient in affliction, and faithful in prayer.

WOW, I wish I had that level of faithful persistence! That level of mature focus! Maybe 3 days ago, I wouldn't have yelled at the wife, scolded the dog, slammed the door on the kids, reacted to a stupid motorist, whined about my Christian fellowship, lamented today's headlines, or commented on the neighbors irritating my otherwise platitude life.

I don't know what it is about this now almost 9th-decade existence, but experience has led to major distrust. My cell phone is now invaded by numerous notifications for services from my automobile to my home services to my body. They are all useless to me at this point, but nonetheless, continue. I have two slots for these irritations with the categories: SPAM and TRASH! My physical mailbox would needs-be checked once monthly for key items from license tags to Amazon books, but must be emptied weekly regardless of whether I need tooth cleaning, Home cleaning, or hearing aids.

Soooooo, back on topic! As a Christian, I can trust and be joyful. If I'm a Christian, why aren't I living in trust and with joy? Is that what Paul is referring to in Romans 7? If I do break trust, is it me or Him? Is he the ROCK ETERNAL? I guess that answers the question. How many issues do we carry personally? Ask your counselor. If we took it up to God's level, might we see resolution from God's perception that we don't envision at our level of thinking? I think yes!

What about JOY? Let's reverse that verse 12. Try being faithful in prayer first. I penned a brief about Google-ing God. We think nothing of taking any question about any item, to Google. It always has an answer. How about doing that with our Creator? He hears it all and answers everything. Don't wait until your sinking 20 feet from the raft and can't swim. Next, "be patient in affliction." How does that work if you're a Christian in N Korea, Iran, or Sudan? Maybe it's more difficult in Gilbert, Arizona. And then, "be joyful in HOPE." Hope is what our faith gives us. Use it, or lose it! Reread Revelation 21 and 22 again.

So turn over a new leaf in your Christian life today. Help put counseling out of business where it should be. Use that room for child care as the young quit worrying about careers and dial into trust as they become "fruitful and multiply" (Genesis 1:28). Put God's guidance first. Solomon wishes he had (Ecclesiastes).

TRUST AND BE JOYFUL ☺

TRUSTING IN GOD'S JOY 2021

As I read a couple daily devotionals last week, they encouraged my faith. "Trust in me forever, for I am the ROCK eternal "(Isaiah 26:4), and "Be joyful in HOPE, patient in affliction, and faithful in prayer" (Romans 12:12). WOW, what a mantra for living life. What a formula for active faith. What an encouragement for living through this present culture. It was tough back in the 1st century when Caesar worship, idol worship, and "unknown god" worship were prevalent. Paul was beaten almost to death. Have you lost a business, lost a house, or been told you can no longer work for a firm?

Idols were big business in those days. If you went up against the program, as Paul did, you were attacking an industry, and not just a religion. Have things changed? As I share this, we are up against a huge and promoted pandemic. Messages from large governments, to large pharmacies, to the enormous information processing system (TV, Internet, Books and Magazines), the pressure is on in seeming overreach. Fewer people die from this pandemic than auto accidents, the flu, or cancer, but you wouldn't think so. (Google it)

God has used natural disasters since the beginning to wake us up to His majesty and power. Mankind still thinks at some point; they become masters of their own destiny. In history past, it was Babel, the flood, and invasion from nation upon nation, whereas today, it is climate change, global warming, eliminating pandemics, and governing (again). It's still the God-fearing vs. the Godless; nothing has changed.

Being "born-again" and saved by Grace, are words of great encouragement. Trust and Joy are great Christian adjectives. These are words that are a part of the faith mantra. As people of faith in the Creator, we have a life advantage if applied. Our will seems to play heavy as one hears of Christians who can't handle the pressure and succumb to suicide. I find that hard to reason, but it is real and proves, as humans, it can happen.

So I encourage, trust, and am joyful. Look to Christ our Creator (Colossians 1:15-20) for trust. Don't look for joy from this culture (mammon). See God's design and guideposts (10 Commandments). It's a lifelong process but worth the focus. It's a struggle when it conflicts with the culture in your

182

environment. But the last 4 chapters of Revelation speak to the reward of hanging in there.

As the Apostle Paul stated: "To live is Christ, to die is gain" (Phil 1:21)

So go live a little, or a lot ☺ the gain comes later, and FOR SURE!

UNITY: A REALITY OR GOAL 2021

This past week our pastor, Costi, shared from 1Peter 3:8-9, "To sum up, let all be harmonious, sympathetic, brotherly, kindhearted, and humble in Spirit; not returning evil for evil, or insult for insult, but giving a blessing instead." This comes right after the section on husbands and wives getting along. This all goes back biblically to the beginning of God's creation when Adam went along with Eve, instead of Eve going along with Adam. Think about it!

This past week I watched an interview show starred by Eric Metaxas on TV. He was interviewing Francis Chan, a well-known Christian pastor, and author. He has a new book out on th e same subject, "Until Unity." I ordered it. FC graduated from Master's Seminary, led a mega-church in Simi Valley, California, and resigned to lead street ministry in San Francisco. It seems, therefore, to be a concern of pastors of the Christian faith. I wrote another brief on this and compared this societal segment to ice cream flavors.

As to unity, the only agreement we Christians have seems to be on the gospel, as rendered in 1 Corinthians 15. After that, the faithful split up on baptism, giving, prosperity, healing, speaking in tongues, and eschatology. So what is Peter saying here, and why? Look at those admonitions closely. They all deal with interpersonal relationships. Maybe we should take a look at the "works" of these ministries. In John 5:36, Christ stated He could be judged based on His "works." Can a Christian be a Christian without works? Can an orange tree be an orange tree without oranges?

So I personally believe Christian unity is purified by its focus on the Rock of Salvation. After that, it's a crap shoot. Christians focus on all sorts of issues and ministries; some have a keen drive to fellowship, or others run the church like a movie theater, with their weekly get-together for an entertaining dose of theology. Some key in on church expansion and open growth groups and new fellowship gatherings. Some jump in a shoe box and remain there for the duration.

Ephesians 4:13 sets the goal. "Until we all attain to the unity of the faith, and of the knowledge of the Son of God, to a MATURE man, to the measure of the stature which belongs to the fullness of Christ." GET IT? Go find a Christian with whom you disagree. Work it out. Set a ministry goal together

184

to get people saved. Perform it down your street, do it in the next town, or do it in Africa. Just don't do anything based on human disagreement, even when you consider a fellowship has bad theology, as opposed to false theology.

Is unity important? In a world where 80% of the inhabitants ignore or hate God? I think so. GET TOGETHER a team and GET MATURE. That's what Paul (and God) is asking for.

WEATHER, THE BIBLE, AND GOD 2021

A friend asked me to do a "1-Page Brief" the other day on the weather. In my mind, I thought, "Are you crazy?" We live in Arizona for this leg of the trip, and summer weather is two-fold: hot and hotter. Rain is no issue; if you want rain just wait two years (or move to the SE or NW USA). And then, I thought about it, and realized that this topic is at the heart of who God is, and our level of faith. WOW, that's dramatic.

I shared with my grandkids years ago, what I feel to be the most important verse in the Bible: Genesis 1:1; God began it all, and created it all. The Bible is also replete with verses saying God continues to be involved, from the Noahdic flood to the confrontation between Moses and Pharaoh. Although God seems to let us meander through life, making one stupid move after another, He has stepped in at key moments to "save" His faithful from total calamity.

Nowhere is this better demonstrated than with Elijah, the prophets of Baal, and King Ahab, in 1 Kings: 17 and 18. You see, we are now getting down to the crux of the matter on faith and reality. Is the Scripture really God's Word? Is it explicit? Is the veracity of God's Word truly infallible?, or should I believe my friends, teachers, professors, and Congress people when it comes to evolution and global warming? Elijah had no qualms about it.

Elijah had called for 3 years of drought as God led him. In a play for supremacy and power, King Ahab had a contest. The Baal prophets went first with everything they could muster, including bloody self-flagellation. It didn't work as they attempted to have their god start a fire. Elijah went second. He stacked wood, dug a ditch around it, poured water all over it 3 times to fill the ditch, and called on God, who consumed the wood and water with fire. It's a great read. They then took the 450 Baal prophets down the hill and slaughtered them all. Sort of like second place in the Super Bowl; NOT.

We now live in one of history's most Godless times and cultures. Our only "escape to reason" are the scriptures. It is only through study and teaching of the Bible, we can learn the TRUTH. Is it really OK to murder unborn babies? Is creation really a colossal accident in time and space without any planning? Is time eternal? Was Jesus Christ a real historical person, or just another religious fable?

So is the weather important? I say yes. Is the weather controlled by its Creator? I say yes. Is the weather predictable? I say to a small degree. Does the Scripture (God's Word) detail these definitions and perspectives? ABSOLUTELY!

So the weather is key. How do we view it? Do we see it as God's painted canvas, as He holds the brush? Or do we also depend on man's ingenuity to overcome God's latest work of art: a drought, a flood, a pruning? We're born helpless. At what point do we become masters of our own destinies? I think never! However, in all we hear and are taught, the lead position is to expunge our Creator God from our perspective. Of course, we have a role, as Christ taught in the parable of the talents. Do your part, but never forget the God who created the opportunity.

GOD BLESS YOUR EFFORT! ☺

WEATHER AND THE BIBLE, PART 2 2021

Is your life one of the puffy clouds against the azure blue skies in the daytime or one of mostly ominous dark bellowing clouds bringing the storms? Early in our marriage, we lived in Chicago. Chicago was a constant storm. Blowing in from the NW across Lake Michigan to the EAST, I noticed it as I constantly traveled for two years. The planes could always take off in those days, but the landing was a whole different thing. One could circle the airport for hours, waiting their turn to break through and land.

The Bible story of Noah is a great example of weather and mankind, and the Creator's power and intervention. There are numerous statements by God in the scriptures where He says He demonstrates His power and Godliness through the natural. Romans 1 is a good read on that. Noah was 500 years old when God had him construct the ark. The ark was larger than a football field. You might call it the "Noahdic Titanic." It took 120 years for him to build it. There must have been quite a team of workers on the construction crew. They still didn't get the message.

We don't know exactly what God had in mind, but the whole world changed in that period. The atmosphere changed. I'm guessing the tectonic plates shifted, everyone except for Noah's family was killed (drowned), and the remake of civilization was reborn. God said He wouldn't eliminate the world again by flooding it "while the earth remains." He gave us the rainbow as a reminder of that fact with most storms (chap 9:12-17). He established a covenant (the Rainbow) with "all flesh" that mankind would never again be destroyed by a universal flood.

In 2nd Peter 3, He explains how the physical world will end and be dissolved. WOW, that's scary. The God of Creation, the God of the Bible, is an amazingly powerful Being in charge of our (and the universe) destiny.

The story of Noah is covered in Genesis 6-9. It's worth the read. The Biblical fact that God controls the weather is a key principle in our faith. Global warming is just another man-made invention for the God-less, just like evolution. How does mankind control its own destiny? Have you been fooled? Have you been educated to believe that life could be/exist, without a Creator? Please understand that all these ideas exist because there is a large and growing contingent hell-bent on persuading the masses that the Bible is folklore and not reality. You find these Godless expositors today in the educational realm, for the most part.

So why is the consideration for weather, a key to the faith of mankind? Because the Bible says, God created it, and controls it. He creates droughts, and He creates floods. He controls growth and vegetation, and He can destroy with it. A loving God has provided for us. But what of our rejection? For believers, we pray and thank God daily for His providence, control of the elements, and sustenance. For unbelievers, the weather will ultimately be a crushing blow of reality.

Joshua 24:15 "choose this day whom you will serve,",,, "but as for me and my house, we will serve the Lord."

WHERE ARE THE DEACONS? (2021)

Three key passages will outline the positions needed to properly operate a Christian church fellowship. We will touch on these for our "one-page briefs" here, but volumes have been written on the subject. In any collegiate type ministry, the most significant aspects will be servant, shepherd, and eldership, to nurture the flock that God intends to "grow." With proper structure, grazing, tending, and weeding, a healthy fellowship can flourish. Time and experience have shown these flocks to come and go. This then proves the need to recognize a structure shown in scripture for the proper guidelines

The 3 scripture locations for a Christian church servant, shepherding, and eldership then are:

Ephesians 4, Acts 6, and 1Timothy 3.

In Ephesians 4 the offices of evangelists, shepherds, and teachers are listed as well as others. These are noted positions "to equip, the saints for the work of the ministry," to build unity and knowledge in the Body of Christ."

In Acts 6, it is noted the Apostles/Elders were overworked and asked for Deacons to be assigned to a table setting so the Elders could focus on their studies and prayer. I think the conclusion isn't that they were looking to get the busywork handled only, but these important positions were significant servants/deacons in building and guiding the flock. They simply had a different focus or set of assignments. The most notable was Stephen (my idol deacon), who was martyred for his faith.

1Timothy 3 then covers the qualifications for one becoming a deacon. These men are called to be "blameless," and their wives "dignified." The verses from 8-13, list their personalities and dedication, demonstrating these are not secondary positions for a church's servant/leadership.So this living organism fellowship called the church has a number of called-out individuals to manage the activities, preach the Gospel, and perform the work of the ministry.

Certain books are classics. One such example was written 5 decades previously, and is appropriately entitled "Body Life," by the late author Dr. Ray Stedman. This excellent treatise was developed from his church history

THANKSGIVING/THANKFULNESS 2021

It's November again, and in the USA, that means we're reminded to be thankful again. FOR WHAT? If you have to ask, you are not aware of the downfall of a society caused by prosperity and the loss of historical knowledge. A historian once stated that "those who neglect history are condemned to repeat it." The study of successful empires/countries is from conquest, to prosperity, to defense (protection of riches they gained), to the ultimate destruction from within and without.   P.S. The Bible is loaded with history.

In the United States, our history notes that in the early days, when our forefathers stopped to celebrate after the first "fall" harvest, as up to that time, life was harsh. The settlers of early times had no grocery stores to visit, had lost many to death from disease, and were just pleased to be alive and eating vegetables and fruit for the first time. I'm upset when the grocer is out of corn ears or my favorite pie filling. I swear the teenagers today think vegetables grow in their local store.

Being thankful, then, stems from an early appreciation for God's Creation, both corporate and personal. Today, I'm grateful for everything, especially my birth and development as a healthy human. That attitude, however, grew exponentially after I appreciated being Born-Again. Since over 80% of mankind doesn't recognize the God of the Bible, and His Son, Jesus Christ, you can see how the average person isn't thankful. FOR WHAT?

In 1863 our country needed healing. It was needed between the cultures of North and South, and between politicians of North and South. How about physically (war wounds from bullets to amputation; and it was gross) for both North and South? So that great Christian President, Abraham Lincoln, set aside a day for Thanksgiving, in November, to help heal our great country. Do your children or grandchildren know that?

Scripture is detailed and explicit; be THANKFUL! 1 Thessalonians 5:18 "In everything give thanks; for this God's will for you in Christ Jesus." Does Paul/God need to say more? What shall I leave out? Does my personal list include poverty, bad health, irritations in life, or death? I think you can get God's picture; in EVERYTHING! In Psalms 95:2, we are exhorted:" Let us come before His presence with THANKSGIVING."

at Peninsula Bible Church in Palo Alto, California, back in the 1960s. It is a great manual and commentary based on the book of Ephesians. Other authors such as John MacArthur and Larry Richards come to mind, but this book is practical application as well as academically palatable.

And so you have it. Some churches have Elders only. Some churches have deacons alone. Some churches have a pastor alone, doing everything. A flourishing church fellowship, however, needs leaders, shepherds, and servants, to do the work of the ministry. Periodically, God sets up great ministries and fellowships. They are a lot of fun and a blessing. They focus on the Gospel in the teaching; people are saved as they see their sin, children are nurtured, and old people are cared for and served. A Biblically organized fellowship can easily handle the growth God sends. A Biblically organized church can perform ministries to their neighborhood, community, and the World. There are many fellowships out there doing just that, as our pastor proves by praying for a different one each week.

GOD BLESS OUR GROWTH!

WISDOM 2021

My friend Chris recently shared a teaching on Wisdom for our men's fellowship. His base was the Book of James, and the sharing of time at tables allowed us to hear from each other about our use of God's wisdom in our lives at home, work, and with friends and neighbors. It's one thing to get wisdom, as James would say, and it's another thing to use and share it, as Jesus would say in the Gospels.

My core takeaway out of 5 refresh topics was the focus on two types of wisdom: Earthly and Heavenly. Nowhere is this better exemplified than in the life of Solomon. He was given a boatload of earthly wisdom, but also blessed with heavenly wisdom concurrent to that. Somewhere along life's path, as He was blessed, by God, with building the New Temple, he picked up 700 wives, and 300 playmates; doesn't sound too WISE to me. He was loaded with POWER, PRAISE, and POSSESSIONS.

So then "Earthly" wisdom might be ascribed to Bezos, Gates, or Musk today. They have created trillions of dollars in assets with what they have created in the business market by 2020. Three of the world's richest have just flown into space. None of them thanked God for the created universe or their particular blessings in this life. Nothing new, my friend! That's why God gave us the Old Testament stories. Pharaoh was a pretty wealthy dude, prior to meeting God through Moses. When the Jews left Egypt, he was broke and dead.

So then, "Heavenly" wisdom came with Jesus Christ. He gave up His power, had no possessions, and sought no praise for the good (miracles) that He did while on earth. That rather changed in Acts 1 when He re-appeared to believers, having been resurrected from death, and took off into the clouds like a rocket ship (no fuel necessary). What Jesus and His disciples had to say about His wisdom in the gospels was earth-shattering,

What James had to say in James 3:13-18 basically covers the subject. James is the NIKE book; just "do it"! It covers the results of using heavenly or earthly wisdom. Wisdom starts with the thinking, but demonstrates in the application and practicing of it. Read the verses, PLEASE! Especially my Grandkids!

Wanna get started? Psalm 111: 10 "The Fear of the Lord is the beginning of (heavenly) Wisdom"

So get as wise as you can, my reader, but make sure you include the heavenly dimension. There's nothing worse than becoming a wealthy "dead" person. Luke 16:19-31 ☹

WOKE ism vs. CHRISTIANITY 2021

My new friend, Pastor Tim, mentioned his son was preaching in town this week, so I asked where and when. I never thought about what I would say if I didn't care for him or his teaching. Nonetheless, I had nothing to fear. He was trained at Phoenix Seminary, planted a church in Phoenix, then San Francisco, then Seattle, now Los Angeles, and has 5 kids. In Seattle, he worked out at a gym full of homosexuals owned and managed by Christians, which has now been closed by the clientele. I like guys that have been around and have life experiences. He seems to be a rubber meets the road pastor.

He began with how the Bible says that it all got started. Genesis 1:1; "In the beginning, God created the universe." The apex of creation then is God creating humans, male and female. In the present climate, humans consider themselves to be the apex as opposed to the created "in the image of God." It all goes downhill from there. Today we see that people actually believe they are what they "feel." Whatever happened to X & Y chromosomes?

I believe I got it correctly as he spoke of autonomy and self-expression in our nature as opposed to created guidance coming from God the Creator. This leads to all sorts of perversion in our current culture, where men are no longer born to be men or women. It's considered in this culture to be a choice to be made as you age, but in a sinful age has been driven to the level of children. They even perform non-reversible surgery on grade-schoolers today. Justin saw it where he lived in the western sub capitols of Satan.

What I gleaned was a message purposed to strike at the folly of created beings to ignore, not know, and deny a (their) Creator. We live in an age of technology that allows for corrections to the natural and the powerful to replace God with the government. If we're not in the last days, we are assuredly in the latter days. I'm sure that Christ is "saddling up"(let the reader be aware).

My extraction/exhortation from his message is that in this WOKE Godless age, anything goes. The pandemic seems to be the accelerant thrown on the fire of a country going in this increasingly Godless direction. Justin's message should be u-tubed, but it would be canceled as inflammatory to non-believers. It does hit the nail on the head, however, that the real and developing battle is the God Fearing vs. the Godless. It's demonstrated in politics today, but even conservative commentators neglect to invoke the fear of God (our Creator).

And one last thought and proposition: LOVE these people, as God loves you. What if you put aside God's LOVE and Grace in your life? "Wretched man that I am" (Romans 7:24). You can hate the sin, but LOVE the sinner

Could it be that Noah's Ark is about to set sail? Could it be time to get out of Lot's Sodom, or leave Jerusalem as Nebuchadnezzar approaches? Lake Mead is dry, New Orleans is flooded, California is burning, and the whole world is shaking. I encourage you, Justin, keep the message flowing. Get ready to duck, however, as Los Angeles is right down the road.

God Bless!

Appendix

Z APPENDIX DEFINED 2021

A quick comment on the appendix I've attached to my "1-PAGE BRIEFS."

I wrote letters to each of my grandchildren at the time of graduation. They couldn't have the same feelings I do, looking back, but seeing them move into their 20s was fun/interesting to me. I barely remember my grandparents and have no earthly idea how they felt about me, if at all.

I did learn of my Dad's testimony before this writing and included that as an influence in my life; I do wish he had shared that, at least at the college level. Maybe he did? ☺

I lastly included the 2 Christian creeds, which sum up my faith and the faith of all true Christians. Upon perusing these appendages, the reader will appreciate from where I'm coming and am motivated to pass on my faith and hope.

It's Harvest Time 2021

The following brief very simply gives a definition to the Christian faith. Firstly we see the Apostle Paul's explanation and definition of the Christian gospel: the GOOD NEWS. It's written to the Corinthians in 1 Corinthians 15. This means nothing to non-Christians. This is followed by the two infamous creeds written in the 300ADs. They are entitled the Apostle's and the Nicene creeds. These are accepted as defining our faith in great detail and are accepted by all Christian denominations today. Finally, you will find common definitions for what we believe and practice in our Christian faith.

Christians tend to disagree on many actions, conclusions, and disciplines in their varying fellowships. They can't disagree on the attached and be Christians. It's that simple; these are the basics of the faith. Paul criticized some for their motivation and actions but was nonetheless pleased as the gospel was being preached (Philippians 1). In this day of mass communication and inordinate prosperity, compared to the past, criticism can be rampant. When we see God touch certain lives, we sometimes can't believe it's real. Instead of rejoicing, we are suspect and critical.

Keep it simple! Learn the basics!

Keep sharing the gospel as best you can. Over 80% of the world doesn't know the gospel. We have a job in front of us. The harvest is ready. We have been blessed with salvation.

My Dear Conner,

I just wanted to give you a quick graduation note. Based on the results, you're a pretty smart fellow. Smart is a combo of intelligence (God Given) and wisdom (your energy and input). I congratulate you and look forward to observing your progress over the next few years. I included a picture of you a few years ago in Jersey when I bought you your first set of clubs ☺. You seemed to take to them, or maybe you were just looking for the candy in the bag. Anyway, it's been fun watching you grow (mature), and WOW, here we are at high school graduation.

Well, you're our #1 grandson, and we love having you even though we don't see much of each other. We included a few more #1's in this note, and we hope it helps with a couple/few tanks of gas. At my graduation, it would have supplied 30-40 tanks. Amazing!

I've also attached a few more ones that could help set your course for college and the future. I've shared 7 of them as that is God's perfect #. If you get to know the Creator while you're studying man's knowledge, the next few, you will be fortunate.

Key # 1's:

Genesis 1, Psalm 1, Proverbs 1, John 1, Galatians 1, Hebrews 1, and Revelation 1

If you read these from time to time, or when you're down, or when you need a pump, you will get God's revelation on who He is, who you are, where everything came from, and where everything is going. That's the most, and best I can give you.

God Bless You. Have a great college experience, and a great life

Love, Chip 2013

Dear Chelsea,

What a joy to honor your request for a new Bible. This one will well replace your children's Bible☺ As you study, you might be surprised at how well the old one covers the basics. This ESV study is the most complete one I've ever seen. I have a friend who studies with me who gave me the same one. It's amazing with maps, comments, and references.

I was 29 when I got interested in God's Word (ll Tim 3:16) (John 1). You have a head start. I'm 74(80 as I write these "1 Page Briefs") now and learning more than ever. It's amazing to realize that God's Word is unfathomable in total; unless and as, the Holy Spirit leads you and opens your eyes. I commented on it the other day, picturing it as a gnat looking at an elephant with visions of eating it all in its lifetime. ☺

The same God/Creator who made the world and universe (Genesis 1:1), and gave you 10 trillion individual DNA cells, gave us this volume of 66 books. People critical of the book don't know it. College professors and fellow students who haven't studied it will be quick to criticize it (see the movie; (God's Not Dead). Most think it a book about dos and don'ts. It's actually full of history, science, and real hope, as well as real Godly LOVE.

Some great readings are John 1, 1 Peter 1, and Psalm 1.

For a great overview, read:

1) Genesis 1-3, where we came from and how we rebelled

2) John 1-3, How God created; repeated, and how we reconcile to our Creator by receiving and being born again

3) Revelation 19-22, Where the world and life is heading; Some to amazing glory and eternal life (US), and some to everlasting punishment, separation from their creator for their rejection of His Love.

You can read this note and give it a look each day, week, month, and year, and then know of what I'm sharing.

God Bless You. You've been a true blessing in our lives

Love Chip Sept 2016

200

My Dear Chandler,

I have but one last piece to complete my first potential of a published book. I've written 100+ "1 Page Briefs" with you and your siblings in mind to learn the Bible. I dedicated it, therefore, to you three, not neglecting my wife, children, or other family, but just wanting to express, share, and help anyone who had questions about God's Word, and to better understand it from what I've learned since I was 28 or 30. That last piece is, as I wrote to your brother and sister as they graduated, will be a part of the appendix of my Book (?).

I'm striving to put together a finished document and realized a note to you was the only missing piece. Did you ever finish a puzzle, and realize you were but one piece away? I think of the first 10 verses of Luke 15, and the parables of the lost sheep, and lost coin. Both the shepherd and the women rejoiced when they "found" the one thing they had lost. This morning I rejoiced as I found the fit with my letter to you.

In church, we sang the song "It is well," and I thought of you and the wall poster in your college room. What an amazing story of faith in God that was! Pastor Chuck then taught Ecclesiastes 12 beginning: "Remember your Creator in the days of your youth before the evil days come...." Verse 13 & 14 states: "the conclusion, when all has been heard is: "FEAR GOD AND KEEP HIS COMMANDMENTS," for God will bring every act to judgment, everything which is hidden, whether it is good or evil." We laughed as Pastor Chuck quoted verse 12: "devotion to books is wearying to the body," (relating to upcoming finals) since this church is located off of the ASU campus and many students were present.

So Ecclesiastes 12 then is a bit of a send-off to the entirety of my book. Ecclesiastes was written, you know, by the wealthiest man ever, with the most power and the most personal freedom to do whatever he wanted (King Solomon). His conclusion was that including your Creator in all that you do will be the hallmark for success. However, excluding your Creator will lead one to a life of vanity, meaninglessness, and vapor. I will guarantee you that life does process as a vapor (looking back ☺).

So your life is just beginning, as our lives are moving on. God bless you, Chandler. You've been a blessing to us, and will be to others that you touch. I know you will do well in this life, but hearken to Solomon's words. You aren't the first to trudge the path. Include God as you move forward, and enjoy the life He leads you through.

LOVE, CHIP 2022

The Apostle's Creed

I believe in God,

the Father Almighty,

Creator of Heaven and earth;

and in Jesus Christ, His only Son, Our Lord,

Who was conceived by the Holy Spirit,

born of the Virgin Mary,

suffered under Pontius Pilate,

was crucified, died, and was buried.

He descended into Hell.

The third day He arose again from the dead;

He ascended into Heaven,

sitteth at the right hand of God, the Father Almighty;

from thence He shall come to judge the living and the dead.

I believe in the Holy Spirit,

the holy Catholic Church,

the communion of saints,

the forgiveness of sins,

the resurrection of the body,

and the life everlasting. Amen.

Nicene creed

We believe in one God,

the Father almighty,

maker of heaven and earth,

of all things visible and invisible.

And in one Lord Jesus Christ,

the only Son of God,

begotten from the Father before all ages,

God from God,

Light from Light,

true God from true God,

begotten, not made;

of the same essence as the Father.

Through him all things were made.

For us and for our salvation

he came down from heaven;

he became incarnate by the Holy Spirit and the virgin Mary,

and was made human.

He was crucified for us under Pontius Pilate;

he suffered and was buried.

The third day he rose again, according to the Scriptures.

He ascended to heaven

and is seated at the right hand of the Father.

He will come again with glory

to judge the living and the dead.

His kingdom will never end.

And we believe in the Holy Spirit,

the Lord, the giver of life.

He proceeds from the Father and the Son,

and with the Father and the Son is worshiped and glorified.

He spoke through the prophets.

We believe in one holy catholic and apostolic church.

We affirm one baptism for the forgiveness of sins.

We look forward to the resurrection of the dead,

and to life in the world to come. Amen.

STATEMENT OF MY DOCTRINAL BELIEF
Homer Kennedy Shafer

I believe in **GOD** as an ever present reality, Infinite and Eternal, but manifest to humanity as Father through Jesus Christ. I think of God as the supreme Personality of the Universe, a purely spiritual power who created and preserves all things. He has manifested Himself to mankind in many ways all down through the ages, but was revealed to us in true spirit through the life and teachings of Christ. As far as His true nature is concerned, I believe that man can know Him only through a spiritual experience, for the Scriptures tell us "O the depth of the riches both of the wisdom and knowledge of God! How unsearchable are His judgments, and His ways past finding out!"

I believe that **MAN** in his creation was fashioned after the image of God in his spiritual nature. He was endowed with power of free will being able to choose between the good & the evil, and that Sin came into the world with man so that all men have sinned & come short of the state of true Righteousness. Since man's fall, all men are born in sin & can be redeemed only through belief in God through Christ with a consecration of life & purpose.

I believe in **JESUS CHRIST** as the Son of God manifest in the Flesh. I believe that because of God's love for the world, Christ was sent to assume the likeness of man in his sin and yet to remain without sin. He was obedient of his own will to death, the death of the cross, and in his resurrection proved himself a victor over sin and the grave. I believe in Him as a true historical personality who ministered to the needs of mankind performing many wonderful works among those who followed Him. One whose life was so perfect that it has become the highest standard that mankind may strive to follow in their quest for truth and uprightness. I believe that the reality of His life still manifests itself today in vital union with the hearts of those who believe in Him through the abiding presence of the Holy Spirit.

I believe in the **HOLY SPIRIT** as the abiding presence of God in man, dwelling in us as a source of wisdom, a witness to the reality of our spiritual experience, a comforter, teaching, imparting hope and love and power, revealing the things of God and Christ, and guiding into a better understanding of truth. It is sent from the Father and convinces of sin and of its inevitable judgment.

I believe in the **BIBLE** comprising the Old and New Testaments as the progressive revelation of God to mankind, written by men and inspired by the Spirit of God. It is the best instruction book available for guidance in the Christian life being a record of the experiences of mankind in his quest for fellowship with the Divine and the best way of life.

I believe that the **KINGDOM OF GOD** is the sovereign sway of the Spirit of God in the hearts and souls of men, an experience entered into by those who have definitely consecrated themselves in life and service to Christ. God's kingdom is righteousness and peace and joy in the Holy Spirit, and we are instructed to pray and seek for it overcoming hatreds, malice and selfishness, establishing world peace and brotherhood, sharing with our fellow men that the Kingdom may become a reality upon earth with the living Christ as its head. Only as these things are realized and practiced in the world can the Kingdom of God become a truly vital force in the life of the individual and in the larger field of the social order and be established in its perfect state.

Z APPENDIX POPS TESTIMONY 2

I believe that mankind may find **SALVATION** from the force and power of sin in their lives. This experience is offered freely to all but is conditioned upon repentance and faith in Christ, "that whosoever believeth in Him should not perish, but have eternal life". However, though vitally important, I believe that this initial experience is only a small part of the program of righteous living for as Paul says there must be a constant striving to overcome the weaknesses of human nature and a progressive climbing toward perfection.

I believe in universal or general **ATONEMENT** as a reconciliation between God and man accomplished by Jesus in his life, death, and resurrection, whereby all who sincerely and humbly repent and truly believe find release from the burden of sin. I am led to believe through reading the Scriptures that this is the one fundamental requisite to Human salvation for we are given to understand that "neither is there Salvation in any other for there is none other name under heaven given among men, whereby we must be saved."

I believe in **REGENERATION** as the change in the moral and spiritual nature of man wrought by the Holy Spirit by which that man comes into a new experience of life, and, thereafter desires to seek after righteousness and the love of God rather than sin and selfish desires. It is one of the fundamental requirements for a vital communion with God for the words of Christ tell us plainly that "ye must be born again" and "except a man be born again, he cannot see the Kingdom of Heaven".

I believe in **JUSTIFICATION** as an act of God by which those who have repented of their sins are released from the sting of spiritual death and restored to their place in the Kingdom. This is a change wrought in man's relation to God, and its roots are found in the love of the Father for the sinful human race. The Scriptures speak of the necessity of it in hearty repentance from sin, surrender of one's self to God, persistent endeavor to keep perfectly His commandments, and humble and sincere trust in the mercy of God through Christ. "God in Christ reconciling the world unto Himself", as Paul speaks of it.

I believe in **PRAYER** as a means of communication with God and as an expression of man's dependence upon God, for all things. I believe that prayer made according to the will of God is efficacious, and that its results are manifested in the objective and subjective experiences of the individual believer. I believe that it is absolutely essential to a real Christian experience and that man can progress spiritually only in so far as he gives though and time to his prayer life.

I believe in the **GOSPEL CHURCH** spoken of in the scriptures as the entire body of believers composed of those living according to the teachings of Christ. It is built and established upon the foundation of belief in Christ as the Savior of the world, and its duties are outlined and defined in the Epistles of Paul. I believe in the spirit of Christian Missions in carrying the Gospel into the uttermost parts of the world "preaching it to every creature according to the command of the Master, but in the spirit of Christ and not on a competitive or economic basis. At present I believe there is a need for a drastic reorgan-ization and revamping of method which shall eliminate the dictatorial and strict denomina-tional aspect and stress rather the spirit of cooperation and service.

I believe in the **LORD'S SUPPER** as an outward ordinance to be observed by all Christians in remembrance of Christ's death and sacrifice, "this do, as oft as ye do it, in remembrance of me". It is a symbol of continuous dependence of the believer for all spiritual life upon the once crucified and now living Savior to whom he is thus united.

I believe that **CHRISTIAN BAPTISM** by immersion in water of a believer in Christ in the name of the Father, Son, and Holy Spirit is a symbol received by the Lord himself in the Jordon. It signifies belief in the death, burial, and resurrection of Christ, and testifies to our willingness to be buried with Him in death to sin and to be raised again in newness of life.

I believe that the **CHRISTIAN SABBATH**, the first day of the week, was ordained by God to be a day set aside for man's benefit and rest that he might have better opportunity therein to worship God.

I believe in **IMMORTALITY** as revealed in the Holy Scriptures as being that state to which the soul of Christian man attains when his journey of the natural life is completed. It is an eternal and spiritual state in which man receives his promised heritages and where he is to abide forever with the Lord apart from evil and all carnal things.

In conclusion, I desire to say that I believe Christianity is still, as ever of old, the spiritual fulfillment of living. the more complicated life grows, the more necessary and inclusive become that spiritual interpretation and fulfillment. Christianity rightly emphasizes the spirit of life, the soul of humanity, the aims of life over and above mechanisms by means of which we live. And the time will never come when such emphasis will not be needed.

I am determined in life and in my ministry to constantly seek a new discovery of God which will release within my life new springs of power such as men in the past have discovered when they rediscovered the religion of Jesus. And as I continue my labors in this challenging life work, I desire that my prayer shall ever be that which the poet has written:

> "From compromise and things half-done
> Keep me, with stern and stubborn pride:
> And when, at last, the fight is won,
> God, keep me still unsatisfied."

Nicene Creed

I believe in one God, the Father Almighty, Maker of heaven and earth, and of all things visible and invisible.

And in one Lord Jesus Christ, the only-begotten Son of God, begotten of the Father before all worlds; God of God, Light of Light, very God of very God; begotten, not made, being of one substance with the Father, by whom all things were made.

Who, for us men for our salvation, came down from heaven, and was incarnate by the Holy Spirit of the virgin Mary, and was made man; and was crucified also for us under Pontius Pilate; He suffered and was buried; and the third day He rose again, according to the Scriptures; and ascended into heaven, and sits on the right hand of the Father; and He shall come again, with glory, to judge the quick and the dead; whose kingdom shall have no end.

And I believe in the Holy Ghost, the Lord and Giver of Life; who proceeds from the Father [and the Son]; who with the Father and the Son together is worshipped and glorified; who spoke by the prophets.

And I believe one holy catholic and apostolic Church. I acknowledge one baptism for the remission of sins; and I look for the resurrection of the dead, and the life of the world to come. Amen.